SEO 2016

& Beyond

Search engine optimization will never be the same again!

By Dr. Andy Williams

ezSEONews
Creating Fat Content

5th Major Version
Updated: 4th September 2015

What People Have Said About Versions of This Book

The original version of this book was published in 2012. That's when the SEO upheaval started with Google moving the goal posts. I updated and re-released major versions of this book in 2013, 2014 and 2015. The copy you have in your hands now is the updated version for 2016. This edition includes my SEO Checklist, which was previously published as a separate book.

The following comments are from customers over this timespan and may refer to any one of the major versions released since 2012.

What everyone is saying:

"Read this book and anything else you can get your hands on by this guy."

"Dr. Andy Williams is, to my mind, the man to listen to when it comes to the subject of building a website in a clean ethical manner. His explanations of what Google, and the other search engines, consider as part of the ranking process cannot be bettered. If you wish to create a long lived website that does not need to fear the latest Google update(s) then pay heed." **Jim**

"A MUST READ for SEO professionals who need to get themselves updated" **Bryan Grandy**

"Five Stars - game changer ,eye opener" **Nahum Pierre**

"After 10 years online, building and promoting websites, I became quite adept at SEO (both on-page and off), but that was then and this is now! Having read this eBook from cover to cover, I think you would be hard pressed to find more informative, descriptive, and easy-to-understand material on the subject of present day SEO anywhere." ~ **Andy Aitch**

"This is the right way to build websites. There is a lot of rubbish written by many so-called experts, but this is not one of them. If you want to learn the best way to do SEO, then this is the leading book I have read, and I have read many." ~ **Dobsy "Dobsy" (UK)**

"Basically I loved this book and highly recommend it. It is the best couple of bucks you will ever spend. It is easy to read, succinct, and brilliant. He offers a lot of great tips without all the fluff that some authors throw in to add page count. Thanks Andy for a good read that upped my SEO IQ." ~ **Nicole Bernd**

"Since Google's Penguin update was released in April 2012, SEO has been turned on its head. Creating themed content with Latent Semantic Indexing (LSI) in mind, instead of keyword focused content, is now the way forward.

Amazingly, this is exactly what Andy has been teaching for the past ten years. I only wished I had known him when I started out in internet marketing. His style of teaching is the best. He's a very genuine and generous person, so if you've been hit by Panda or Penguin, then this book is exactly what you need." ~ **Carole**

"Great book, super helpful, and makes SEO easy to understand, especially for an ecommerce novice! I would definitely recommend this to anyone trying to get a handle on best practices in SEO." ~ **cswaff**

"Andy was warning of a Panda type hit at least two years before the Panda was born. Although the Penguin update has changed things more than a bit, in this book, Dr Andy clearly, and in simple terminology, explains the strategies and tactics needed to stay on the good side of Google." ~ **Tony Crofts**

"Great at teaching the difference in old SEO practices Vs. new techniques." ~ **Ms. WriterGirl**

"Andy is one of the few people that I listen to when it comes to SEO. Rather than "follow the usual crowd", that tends to share rehashed information with little value that's based on fact, Andy does his own testing to determine what is actually working for him, and then shares his own results." ~ **J. Stewart**

"This book was a very quick and easy read from start to finish. I found it to be an excellent work with some very mature insights into the nuances of how to get in good graces with Google. It took a few of my beliefs and approaches to Search Engine Optimization and turned them upside down." ~ **Jonathan W. Walker**

"This is groundbreaking Internet marketing information. Stuff you won't find elsewhere. Being a long-time pupil of Dr. Andy, I have put much of it to the test myself and I know it proves out. If you are in the Internet business, you need to read this book." ~ **Norman Morrison**

"After following Andy Williams for over 8 years now, I had a hunch his new SEO book would be a winner . . . and it is. It's simple, straight forward, and on target with respect to the latest updates, upgrades, and algorithmic mods by our friends at Google. Do what Andy teaches, especially with reference to great content creation, and you will be successful in your SEO efforts." ~ **Chris Cobb**

Contents

How to Use This Book

This book divides into two main sections.

The first section is a complete overview of "White Hat" SEO. White Hat SEO is the kind of SEO that Google actually approves of and wants you to carry out on your website. This is because it helps both Google and your site visitors to better understand the content.

Since Google's Panda and Penguin updates, it really isn't worth employing "Black Hat" or even "Grey Hat" techniques, unless of course you are happy going to bed in the knowledge that your site may be gone in the morning, and without warning.

The second section of this book tries to help you identify areas on your site that are causing you ranking problems, or even a penalty. The comprehensive checklist will take you through a number of tests that you can carry out on your own site(s). These tests make sure you're not venturing over to the dark side.

The checklist has 10 main sections, each one looking at a different aspect of your website. If your site has been struggling to rank, or has dropped back in the rankings, the idea is to work your way through all 10 sections, correcting issues as you go.

Each section will tell you what you need to be looking out for as well as the theory behind why you need to make these checks. Each chapter ends with a bulleted "checklist" that you can tick off as you go along.

At the end of section two, you will find a master checklist that includes all of the checkpoints mentioned throughout that section of the book.

A Note About Page Rank (PR)

If you have never heard of Page Rank before, here's a short introduction.

Every page on the internet has something called Page Rank, more commonly known as PR or PageRank. PR is an algorithm used by Google Search that helps to rank websites in their search engine result pages (SERPs). "PageRank" was named after Google co-founder Larry Page. It is measured on a logarithmic scale from 0-10. A new page will have a PR0. Actually it won't be zero, but "Unranked", which is very close to zero. Note that Google may still index unranked pages.

When page 'A' links to page 'B', page 'B' gets an increase in its PR that is a proportion of the PR on page 'A'.

If page 'A' has a PR of zero, then page 'B' gets very little additional PR. However, if page 'A' has a PR of '5', then page 'B' gets a huge boost in its PR status.

If a page has a lot of incoming links, it gathers PR from each of those pages, thus making it more "important". This is where we get the idea of a link being a "vote" for a page. The more incoming links a page has, the more PR it gets, and the more important it becomes. In other words, the page gains in status, or reputation. The more important a page is, the better it will rank in the Google SERPs.

For many years, PR was, and still is to some extent, discussed and debated about in SEO circles. It was once thought of as some kind of ranking Deity. PR was seen as an all-powerful property of a page that could be sculpted and used to make other pages rank better. It was a measure of how important a page was to Google.

The search engine giant even provided a toolbar for webmasters so that they could check the PR for pages on their websites:

https://support.google.com/toolbar/answer/79837?hl=en

For many webmasters, SEO became a game of chasing PR. Getting links pointing back to their sites from other high PR pages was the only thing that mattered.

By giving webmasters the toolbar, Google also gave them the power to rank at will. It allowed them to funnel PR to important pages to give them the ranking power they needed to dominate the SERPs.

However, for the last couple of years Google have been trying to distance itself from PageRank. They have done this in an attempt to convince webmasters that it no longer has an important ranking factor. Google even stopped updating their toolbar so that no one could tell the true PR of a webpage. The last update I am aware of was back in December 2013.

In October 2014, Google's John Mueller said "We are probably not going to be updating it [PageRank] going forward, at least in the Toolbar PageRank".

Clearly that "...at least in the Toolbar PageRank" statement indicates PR is still important to Google. They just don't want webmasters knowing the PR of their webpages as it gives them too much control.

While we do talk about PR a little in this book, there is no emphasis on it. PR is still important in the way that it is accrued. This is because a page with high PR has a lot of good links pointing to it, and is therefore an important page. However, PR no longer has that SEO deity that it once did. With that said, let's get started.

What Is SEO?

SEO stands for **S**earch **E**ngine **O**ptimization. It's best defined as the steps a webmaster takes to increase the visibility of his/her webpages in the search engines organic search results.

OK, let's just define a couple of terms at this point, before moving on.

A "**webmaster**" is simply a person who is responsible for a particular website.

Organic search results are those listings in the SERPs (Search Engine Results Pages) that are there on merit because of their relevance to the search term typed in. It's important to differentiate between organic and paid listings. With paid listings, webmasters pay the search engines to have their pages (in the form of ads) listed at the top of the SERPs.

So the term **SERPs** refers to the **S**earch **E**ngine **R**esults **P**ages, which are the pages of results you get when you carry out any search at any search engine.

Before we go on any further, I should just mention that this book focuses on Google SEO. Google is the largest search engine on the planet. In fact, most search traffic from around the world comes directly from Google Search. Google have become synonymous with the term "search engine". It's an expression that has even found its way into the English dictionary as a verb. I expect you've heard someone describe how they "**googled**" something or other. Google is the most important place to rank well, and if you rank well on Google, chances are you will rank well on Yahoo and Bing too.

Why Is SEO Necessary?

So You Want to Build a Website, Right?

Unfortunately, if you build it, even if it's really impressive, no one will know about you, at least not without some help from the search engines. The sad truth is that you can have the best website on the planet, but if people cannot find you, then cyberspace can be a very lonely place. This brings us back to search engines.

Fact: Search engines are the #1 way people find websites.

The good news is that it is easy to get your pages into the search engines.

The bad news is that it is difficult to get your pages to rank high enough to be visible in the search engines.

A study based on data, taken in July 2014, showed that the page which ranks on page one in position #1 of the SERPs typically gets around 31% of all clicks on that page.

The web page ranked in position #2 gets 14%.

The page in #3 gets 10%. If we look at positions 6-10 combined, they get around 3.7% of all clicks.

Web pages ranked on page two of the search results get around 4% of clicks, and on page 3+, it drops to 1.6% of clicks.

From this information, you can see that it is important to not only rank in Google, but to rank as highly as possible. Even one or two places can mean big drops in potential search engine traffic.

Below is a graph showing values for the click-through rates (CTR) of the top five positions in Google:

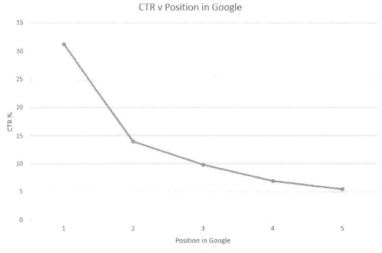

Position 6-10 had a combined CTR of just 3.73%, which was less than the CTR for position 5.

You can read the full report here:

http://www.advancedwebranking.com/google-ctr-study-2014.html

How Do We Rank Pages as High as Possible?

To rank high in the organic search results, your page needs to be one of the best matches for the search term typed into the search engine's search box.

So what makes a page the best match? Well, that is a secret known only to Google, but a little later in this chapter we'll look at some of the factors that Google considers when ranking web pages.

How We Used to Rank Pages

In the good old days (that's up to about 2010), ranking in Google was relatively easy.

You see, at that time Google's algorithm (the complex code that determines where a webpage will rank) was heavily based on the keywords on a page, along with the links from other websites pointing back to it. These were the main ranking factors and webmasters new it. Since both of those factors could be controlled and manipulated by the site owners, many webmasters began to organize and manipulate things so that they could rank well in the SERPs.

Here was the process for doing this:

1. Identify the keywords you want to rank for.

2. Create a page that was "optimized" for that particular keyword or Key phrase. The quality of the content was not important back then. What was important was that you included your chosen keyword or key phrase into as many places as possible (a term aptly named as keyword stuffing). This would typically

include the title of the page, the opening header, in the body of the content (maybe five times or more per 100 words), and in the ALT tags (a text alternative for an image or object on a page). Keywords were often included even in the domain name itself. The more times you could get your term in there, the better the results were.

3. Build backlinks, often by the tens of thousands, using automated back-linking tools. The anchor text for most of the backlinks used the same term(s) we wanted to rank for.

That was it basically. You could rank for literally any term using that simple formula.

Webmasters were able to rank in the SERPs for anything they wanted, for whatever they wanted. Back in the very early days, if you got into the first top 10 positions on page one of Google, you would remain there for three months, until the next update came out.

Google had lost control.

As you can imagine, the SERPs offered poor quality content to web searchers, and that made Google look bad. Obviously Google wanted the best, most relevant results shown to its users. In many cases, spots in the top 10 were filled with trashy content; spammy sites that offered little or no value to the web surfer.

Over time, Google got to refine its algorithm, thus making it more and more difficult for webmasters to game the system. In Google's ideal world, their prized algorithm would be based entirely on factors that webmasters could not control or manipulate.

As you will see later in the book, Google's Panda and Penguin updates (as well as several other major updates) were designed so that the company could start taking back control from the webmasters. By removing the factors that webmasters could control from their algorithm, or giving them less importance, Google made it increasingly difficult to manipulate a web page ranking. Bear this in mind when we look at the top ranking factors later in this chapter for 2015.

Personalized Search Results

In recent years, Google have been applying more and more personalization to the search results. So what does that mean exactly? It means that what you see when you search for a phrase in Google, may not be the same as what someone in a different part of the country would see for the same search term. In fact, it might not even be the same set of results that your neighbour sees, or your mom sitting next to you on the couch while searching on her mobile phone.

It is important to realize this. Not everyone sees the same results for the exact same search query.

You see, when someone searches on Google, the search giant will apply filters to the results in an attempt to show that searcher the most relevant results, based on their own personal circumstances.

As a quick example, let's say you search Google for an antivirus program while using your iMac. The chances are that you'll probably see a bias of anti-virus pages in the SERPs, specifically targeting Mac users. Do the same search on a PC and you'll get PC antivirus software. Repeat the search on an Android phone or iPhone, and you'll get results tailored to those operating systems.

This is one simple example. Google looks at much more than just your operating system. Other factors they'll try to use include:

1. Your location (whether that is your reported location, IP address, or GPS location as given out by mobile devices).

2. Your search history, which looks at what have you been searching for in recent days or weeks.

3. Your social networks, including your likes, your friends and your circles.

4. Whether you are searching on a mobile device, desktop or even SmartTV.

5. Your preferred language.

Personalization of the search results is meant to make our lives easier, and in many ways it does. However, as far as SEO is concerned, personalization can be a pain if we don't know what other people are seeing in their SERPs.

Top Ranking Factors in 2015

Earlier we saw that Google wanted to build its algorithm around quality indicators, ones which were not under webmaster control. In this section we'll look at some of those indicators used by Google. Think about each one in turn, and how much control a webmaster has over it.

Ranking Factors can be split into two groups, namely "on page" and "off page".

On Page Factors

1. Quality Content

Google is looking for high quality content that is relevant to the search query. They will look at the language used on a page, and for terms related to the query. I call these "theme words". Longer pages tend to do better, and the inclusion of photos and/or video works to your advantage too. Furthermore, pics and vids also help to retain the visitor's interest.

2. Page Load Time

Nobody likes waiting around for a page to load. If your web pages are taking five or more seconds to open fully, your visitors may decide not to hang around and hit the back button. According to research, your average web user has an attention span of just a few seconds, less than a goldfish actually. So it's important that your pages load quickly. If the searcher came from Google, a slow page load is bad news for you, since Google sees both the "bounce" and "exit" rates as negatives for your page.

3. Internal Links from Other Pages on the Site

If you look at a website like Wikipedia, you'll see a lot of **internal links** on the pages. Internal links are simply links that go from one page on a website to a different page on the same site. Any links we talk about in this book that link out to other websites are called **external links**. So external Links are simply links that point at (or target) any website other than the one the link exists on (the source). Internal links are there to help the visitor navigate around your website's pages. As someone reads a page on Wikipedia, they might come across a word or phrase they do not understand, or simply want to know more about. By "internally" linking key words or phrases to other pages on Wikipedia, visitors get to navigate around the site more easily and find the information they are looking for quickly.

4. Bounce Rates

We mentioned bounce rates earlier in the context of fast loading pages. A "bounce" is simply a visitor who clicks a link in the SERPs and then returns to Google. The quicker the return, the worse it is for your page as it tells Google the visitor was not satisfied. The higher the percentage of visitors who navigate away from the site, after viewing only one page, the more your reputation suffers in the eyes of Google. After all, if people come to your site and don't bother looking around (navigating to other pages of interest), then this tells Google that your site does little to inspire its visitors.

Let's think how this might work.

Say a visitor on Google searches for "vitamin A deficiency" and visits the first page in the SERP. Not finding what they want, they then click the browser's back button to return to Google. They may then click on another site further down the SERP to see if that can provide what they are looking for.

What does this tell Google about your site?

It tells them that the visitor did not find the information they wanted on your page/site. Google knows this because they returned to the search results and repeated (or refined) their search.

If lots of people around the world search for a certain phrase, and an unusually high percentage of them bounce back from the same webpage that is ranked #1 in Google for the search term, what do you think Google will do?

Doesn't it make sense that they would demote that page in the SERPs - **for that particular search phrase** - since lots of people are not finding it relevant for their search query?

Bounce rates go hand-in-hand with relevance. If visitors find a page relevant for their search query, they'll stay on the page for longer. If they have been impressed by what they found on the first page, then they will also more than likely take time to look around other pages of interest on the same site. This means they've visited more than one page and have not bounced directly back to Google. This tells the search engine that they were pleased with what they found.

5. *Time a Visitor Stays on Your Page / Site.*

Google monitors the time that visitors stay on web pages. One of the ways they do this is through their Google Analytics platform. Google Analytics is a freemium web analytics service for site owners. What it does is track and report on your website traffic. Because it's free, a lot of webmasters install it on their sites. This gives Google the ability to accurately track the site's visitors. It'll track a number of variables including things like time spent on the site, the route a visitor takes through your site, how many pages they visit, what operating system they use, the screen resolution, device they are using, and so on.

Most of the on-page factors are within the control of the webmaster. Even bounce rates and the time the visitor stays on your site is within your control, to a certain extent. If you provide quality content and the rich experience visitor's demand these days, then you'll get lower bounce rates while keeping the visitor on your page/site for longer.

Off Page Factors

1. *Click-through Rates (CTR)*

This is something we should be paying particular attention to. To a certain extent, the CTR is within our control. For anyone who's unfamiliar with CTR, then take a look at this example:

Let's say a web page ranks in position #5 on page one of Google and the folks seem to like that listing in the SERP, with 15% of them clicking on the link. Usually a page listed in position #5 would get around 5% of the clicks. When Google sees more people than expected clicking that link, they will give it a boost in their rankings. After all, it's apparently what the searchers are looking for, and so it deserves a higher slot on the first page.

On the other side of the coin, imagine a spammer (an "official" term used by Google to describe someone trying to manipulate rankings for one of their web pages) manages to bypass Google's algorithm with a "loophole", and ranks #1 for a search term. Remember, in position #1, a link typically gets 31% of the clicks. However, this #1 ranking page only gets 15% because searchers are not impressed with the link title or its description. On top of that, 95% of people who do visit that link bounce right back to Google within 30 seconds or less of clicking the link. Google now has clear user signals that the web page ranking #1 is not popular with searchers. Because of this, Google starts moving the site further down the rankings until it's finally knocked off. This means that bad content will rarely get to the top of Google, and if it does, it won't get to stay there for long.

2. *Social Signals*

Social signals like Google +1s, Tweets, Facebook shares, Pinterest pins, and so on, are clearly used as ranking factors in Google, though very minor ones. Any boost that social signals might offer your site will be short-lived. This is because of the transient nature of "social buzz".

For example, let's say that a new piece of content goes viral and is shared around by thousands of people via social media channels. This is typically done within a relatively short space of time. Google will take notice of this because they realize the content is something visitors want to see, and so they give it a ranking boost. After the social interest peaks and the shares inevitably start to decline, so does the ranking boost in Google.

Social sharing is a great concept and should be encouraged on your site. Even so, don't expect the backlinks created from social channels to give you a big or long-lasting ranking boost, because they won't.

3. Backlinks

When "webpage A" links to "webpage B" on another site, page B gets a "backlink". Google sees this as page A (on site A) voting for page B (on site B). The general idea is that the more "external" backlinks, or "votes", that a page gets from other sites on the web, the more important or valuable it must be.

Today, and probably for the foreseeable future, backlinks remain one of the most important rankings factors in Google's algorithm. However, more is not always better. Let me explain.

A web page that has **dozens** of links from authority sites like CNN, BBC, NY Times, etc, is clearly an important web page. After all, quality, authority sites like the ones above would hardly link to trash.

A page that has **thousands** of backlinks from low quality websites, on the other hand, is most probably not very important at all. Clearly backlinks can be a powerful indicator of a page's value, but just as clear is that not all backlinks are equal. By having hundreds, or even thousands, of low quality backlinks pointing to a single page is a good indicator to Google that webmasters are trying to self-promote their own pages to manipulate the results in the SERPs.

What Google needs to do is "grade" backlinks according to their worth. Backlinks from high quality "authority" web pages will count far more than backlinks from low quality pages/sites. Therefore, a page that gets a lot of high quality backlinks is likely to be able to rank well in Google. A page that has a lot of low quality backlinks, however, will struggle to rank at all. Google may even penalize that page or site for having too many poor quality backlinks, for the reasons mentioned above.

Google's Battle for Survival

Over the years, Google have had to change and adapt to survive. It has been in a constant battle with webmasters who are eager to manipulate its SERPs. Since the algorithm is based on real factors and properties of a website, site owners have been trying to identify those factors and use them to their advantage. Whenever webmasters find a competitive advantage (sometimes called a loophole), Google tries to quickly plug it.

Here's a typical example of this "cat and mouse game" that has being going on between Google and webmasters over the years:

Over a decade ago, webmasters found out that Google used the Meta Keyword tag as a major ranking factor. What did they do? They began stuffing this tag with keywords in an attempt to rank well for those terms. What did Google do? They started to ignore the Meta Keyword tag, effectively closing that loophole.

I would like to point out that I do believe Google still looks at the Meta Keyword tag, but not as you might think. I think the company uses it to help identify spammers. Any page that has a Meta keyword tag stuffed with dozens, or even hundreds, of keywords, is clearly doing something underhand, or at least trying to.

Here is another example of a loophole being closed.

A few years ago, webmasters found out that by using a domain name that essentially consisted of nothing more than the keyword phrase they wanted to rank for, the site would get a massive ranking boost in the SERPs. This type of domain is called an Exact Match Domain (EMD). We'll look at EMDs later. Anyway, in September 2012, Google released the "EMD Update" which removed that unfair ranking advantage. Hundreds of thousands of EMD sites dropped out of the Google top 10 overnight, which saw an end to a large industry that had profited in buying and selling EMDs.

Since an EMD is usually a commercial search phrase, most inbound links to these EMD sites also contained that exact commercial term. This over-optimization for a commercial phrase was bad news for the site owners. This was because Google's Penguin was on the lookout for this exact type of over-optimization.

Today, EMD sites are rarely seen in the top 10 for any mildly competitive search terms.

The battle between spammer and search engine continues to rage on to this today. Spammers find loopholes, and Google plugs them.

In September 2011, Google CEO Eric Schmidt said that they had tested over 13,000 possible algorithm updates in 2010, approving just 516 of them. Although 516 may sound a lot (it's more than one update a day), it certainly wasn't an unusual year. Google probably updates their algorithm at least 500-600 times every year. Most of these updates will be minor, but Google does roll out major changes every now and again. We'll look at the more important ones in the next chapter.

The one thing all Google updates have in common is that they are designed to improve the search results for the people that use the search engine – your potential visitors.

Panda, Penguin and Other Major Updates

We could go back to the very beginning to see all the changes and updates that Google have made, but I want to focus on those changes that have happened since 2011. These are the ones that have changed the way we do SEO today.

Changes in 2011

This was a huge year in SEO terms, shocking many webmasters. In fact, 2011 was the year that wiped a lot of online businesses off the face of the web. Most deserved to go, but quite a few innocent victims got caught up in the shake up too, never to recover.

At the beginning of the year, Google tried to hit scraper sites (sites that used bots to steal and post content from other sites). This was all about trying to attribute ownership of content back to the original owner, and thus penalize the thieves.

On February 23, the Panda update launched in the USA. Panda (also called "Farmer") was essentially targeting low quality content and link farms. Link farms were basically collections of low quality blogs that were set up to link out to other sites. The term "thin content" became popular during this time; describing pages that really didn't say much, and were there purely to host adverts. Panda was all about squashing thin content, and a lot of sites took a hit too.

In March the same year, Google introduced the +1 button. This was probably expected bearing in mind that Google had confirmed they used social signals in their ranking algorithm. What better signals to monitor than their own?

In April 2011, Panda 2.0 was unleashed, expanding its reach to all countries of the world, though still just targeting pages in English. Even more signals were included in Panda 2.0. They probably included user feedback via the Google Chrome web browser. Here users had the option to "block" pages in the SERPs that they didn't like.

As if these two Panda releases were not enough, Google went on to release Panda 2.1, 2.2, 2.3, 2.4, 2.5, and 3.1, all in 2011. Note that Panda 3.0 is missing. There was an update between 2.5 and 3.1, but it is commonly referred to as the Panda "Flux". Each new update built on the one previous, helping to eliminate still more low quality content from the SERPs. With each new release of Panda, webmasters worried, panicked and complained on forums and social media. A lot of websites were penalized, though not all deserved to be; unavoidable "collateral damage" Google casually called it.

In June 2011, we saw the birth of Google's first social network project, Google Plus.

Another change that angered webmasters was "query encryption", introduced in October 2011. Google said they were doing this for privacy reasons, but webmasters were suspicious of their motives. Prior to this query encryption, whenever someone searched for something on Google, the search term they typed in was passed on to the site they clicked through to. That meant webmasters could see what search terms visitors were typing to find their pages using any web traffic analysis tool. Query encryption changed all of this. Anyone who was logged into their Google account at the time they performed a search from Google would have their search query encrypted. This prevented their search terms from being passed over to the websites they visited. The result of this was that webmasters increasingly had no idea which terms people were using to find their sites or site pages.

In November 2011, there was a freshness update. This was to supposedly reward websites that provided time-sensitive information (like news sites), whenever visitors searched for time-sensitive news and events.

As you can see, there was a lot going on in 2011, but it didn't stop here.

Changes in 2012

Again, 2012 was a massive year for SEOs and webmasters. There was a huge number of prominent changes, starting with one called "Search + your World" in January. This was an aggressive measure by Google to integrate its Google+ social data and user profiles into the SERPs.

Over the year, Google released more than a dozen Panda updates, all aimed at reducing low quality pages from appearing in the SERPs.

In January 2012, Google announced a page layout algorithm change. This aimed at penalizing pages with too many ads, very little value, or both, positioned above the fold. The term "above the fold" refers to the visible portion of a web page when a visitor first lands on it. In other words, whatever you can see without the need to scroll down is above the fold. Some SEOs referred to this page layout algorithm change as the "Top Heavy" update.

In February, Google announced another 17 changes to its algorithm, including spell-checking, which is of particular interest to us. Later in the same month, Google announced another 40 changes. In March, there were 50 more modifications announced, including one that made changes to anchor-text "scoring".

Google certainly weren't resting on their laurels. On April 24, the Penguin update was unleashed. This was widely expected, and webmasters assumed it was going to be an over-optimization penalty. Google initially called it a "webspam update", but it was soon named "Penguin". This update checked for a wide variety of spam techniques, including keyword stuffing. It also analysed the anchor text used in external links pointing to websites.

In April, yet another set of updates were announced, 52 this time.

In May, Google started rolling out "Knowledge Graph". This was a huge step towards semantic search (the technology Google uses to better understand the context of search terms). We also saw Penguin 1.1 during this month and another 39 announced changes. One of these new changes included better link scheme detection. Link scheme detection was for the purpose of revealing where webmasters had fabricated links to gain better rankings.

In July, Google sent out "unnatural link warnings" via Google Webmaster Tools, to any site where they had detected a large number of "unnatural" links. To avoid a penalty,

Google gave webmasters the opportunity to remove the "unnatural" links.

Think of unnatural links as any link the webmaster controls, and ones they probably created themselves or asked others to create for them. These would include links on blog networks and other low quality websites. Inbound links such as these typically used a high percentage of specific keyword phrases in their anchor text. Google wanted webmasters to be responsible for the links that pointed to their sites. Webmasters who had created their own sneaky link campaigns were in a position to do something about it. However, if other sites were linking to their pages with poor quality links, then Google expected webmasters to contact the site owners and request they remove the bad link(s).

If you have ever tried to contact a webmaster to ask for a link to be removed, you'll know that it can be an impossible task. So for many webmasters, this was an impractical undertaking, since the unnatural link warnings were often the result of tens or hundreds of thousands of bad links to a single site. Google eventually back-tracked and said that these unnatural link warnings may not result in a penalty after all. The word on the street was that Google would be releasing a tool to help webmasters clean up their link profiles.

When you think about it, Google's flip-flopping on this policy was understandable and just. After all, if websites were going to get penalized for having too many spammy links pointing to their pages, then that would open the doors or opportunity for criminal types. All any dishonest webmasters would have to do to wipe out their competition would be to point thousands of low quality links at their pages using automated link-building software.

Also in July, Google announced a further 86 changes to their algorithm.

In August, the search engine giant started to penalize sites that had repeatedly violated copyright, possibly via The Digital Millennium Copyright Act (DMCA) takedown requests.

For those who might not be familiar with this, the DMCA is a controversial United States digital rights management (DRM) law. It was first enacted on October 28, 1998, by the then-President Bill Clinton. The intent behind DMCA was to create an updated version of copyright laws. The aim was to deal with the special challenges of regulating digital material.

Ok, moving on to September 2012, another major update occurred, this time called the EMD update. You'll remember that EMD stands for Exact Match Domain, and refers to a domain that exactly matches a keyword phrase the site owner wants to rank for. EMDs had a massive ranking advantage simply because they used the keyword phrase in the domain name. This update removed that advantage overnight.

In October of this year, Google announced that there were 65 algorithm changes in the previous two months.

On October 5, there was a major update to Penguin, probably expanding its influence to non-English content.

Also in October, Google announced the Disavow tool. This was Google's answer to the "unnatural links" problem. They completely shifted the responsibility of unnatural links onto the webmaster by giving them a tool to disavow, or deny any responsibility or support for those links. If there were any external links from bad neighbourhoods pointing to your site, and you could not get them removed, you could now disavow those links, effectively rendering them harmless.

Finally in October 2012, Google released an update to their "Page Layout" update, and in December, they updated the Knowledge Graph to include non-English queries in a number of the more popular languages. This drew an end to the Google updates for that year.

Changes in 2013

In 2013, Google updated both Panda and Penguin several times. These updates refined the two different technologies to try to increase the quality of pages ranking in the SERPs. On July 18, a Panda update was thought to have been released to "soften" the effects of a previously released Panda, so Google obviously watched the effects of its updates, and modified them accordingly.

In June, Google released the "Payday Loan" update. This targeted niches with notoriously spammy SERPs. These niches were often highly commercial, which offered great rewards for any page that could rank highly. Needless to say, spammers loved sites like these. Google gave the example of "payday loans" as a demonstration when announcing this update, hence its name.

In July, we saw an expansion of the Knowledge Graph, and in August there was another major update announced by Google.

August 2013 – Hummingbird – Fast & Accurate?

Hummingbird was the name given to Google's latest search algorithm. It was not part of an existing algorithm, or a minor algorithm update, but an entirely brand-spanking new algorithm that was unboxed and moved into place on August 20, 2013 (though it was not announced to the SEO community until September 26).

This was a major change to the way Google sorted through the information in its index. In fact, a change on this scale had probably not occurred for over a decade. Think of it this way. Panda and Penguin were changes to parts of the old algorithm, whereas Hummingbird was a completely new algorithm, although it still used components of the old one.

Google algorithms are the mathematical equations used to determine the most relevant pages to return in the search results. The equation uses over 200 components, including things like PageRank and incoming links, to name just two.

Apparently, the name Hummingbird was chosen because of how fast and accurate these birds were. Although many webmasters disagreed, Google obviously thought at the time that this reflected their search results – fast and accurate.

Google wanted to introduce a major update to the algorithm because of the evolution in the way people used Google to search for stuff. An example Google gave was in "conversation search", whereby people could now speak into their mobile phone, tablet or even desktop browser to find information. To illustrate, let's say that you were interested in buying a Nexus 7 tablet. The old way of finding it online was to type something like this into the Google search box:

"Buy Nexus 7"

However, with the introduction of speech recognition, people have since become a lot more descriptive in what they are searching for. Nowadays, it's just as easy to dictate into your search browser something like:

"Where can I buy a Nexus 7 near here?"

The old Google could not cope too well with this search phrase, but the new Hummingbird was designed to do just that. The old Google would look for pages in the index that included some or all of the words in the search phrase. A page that included the exact phrase would have the best chance of appearing at the top of Google. If no pages were found with the exact phrase, then Google would look for pages that included the important words from it, e.g. "where" "buy" and "nexus 7".

The idea behind Hummingbird was that it should be able to interpret what the searcher was *really* looking for. In the example above, they are clearly looking for somewhere near their current location where they can purchase a Nexus 7.

In other words, Hummingbird was supposed to determine searcher "intent" and return pages that best matched that intent, as opposed to best matching keywords in the search phrase. Hummingbird is still around today and tries to understand *exactly* what the searcher wants, rather than just taking into account the words used in the search term.

On December 2013, there was a drop in the authorship and rich snippets displayed in the SERPs. This was a feature where Google displayed a photo of the author and/or other information next to the listing. However, Google tightened up their search criteria and removed these features from listings.

Changes in 2014

In February 2014, Google updated their page layout update.

In May the same year, Payday Loan 2.0 was released. This was an update to the original Payday Loan algorithm, and was thought to have extended the reach of this algorithm to international queries.

Also in May, Panda was updated, called Panda 4.0).

That brings us up to the current time, as I am writing this book. As you can see, Google have been very active in trying to combat the spam thrown at them. The two major updates that most webmasters worried about, and continue to worry about, are Panda and Penguin. Together, these two technologies weed out low quality pages, and pages that have been engineered to rank highly in the search engines. But as previously noted there are sometimes a few innocent victims that lose out to these updates too, especially in the case of major updates.

That last statement sends shivers down the spines of many webmasters.

Anyone who builds a website will want it to rank well in Google. Without having a high-profile presence in the SERPs, a site won't get much traffic, if any at all. If that happens, webmasters WILL try to boost their rankings, and the traditional way is by working on the "on-page SEO" and inbound links. However, over the last couple of years in particular, Google have introduced measures that aim to penalize any webmaster who is actively trying to boost rankings via traditional SEO methods.

Google wants the best pages to rank at the top of the SERPs for obvious reasons. So Google rewards the pages that deserve to be at the top, rather than pages that webmasters force to the top using SEO (much of which Google collectively calls "webspam").

What this means to you is that you have to deliver the absolute best quality content you can. You need to create content that deserves to be at the top of the SERPs. You know, content is not only King now, but it has always been King. The difference now is that Google algorithms are so much better at determining what constitutes great content and what doesn't. In other words, it's no longer easy to take shortcuts and use underhanded tactics to trick the algorithms as it once was.

Fortunately for you, Google offers a lot of advice on how to create the type of content they want to show up in their SERPs. In fact, they have set up a web page called "Webmaster Guidelines". This tells you *exactly* what they want, and just as importantly, what they don't want. We'll look at this shortly, but first, let's see how we used to create content in the past.

Changes in 2015

The Mobile-friendly Update

On April 21, Google began rolling out an update that was designed to boost mobile-friendly web pages in their mobile search results.

To help webmasters prepare for the update, Google provided a web page where webmasters could test their site to see if it was mobile-friendly or not. You can find the mobile-friendly testing tool here:

https://www.google.com/webmasters/tools/mobile-friendly/

To use this tool, you simply enter your webpage URL and wait for the results. Hopefully you will see something like this:

Mobile-Friendly Test

http://ezseonews.com/

Awesome! This page is mobile-friendly.

The mobile-friendly update:

1. Only affects searches carried out on mobile-devices.

2. Applies to individual pages, not entire websites.

3. Affects ALL languages globally.

This update makes a lot of sense. If someone is searching on a small screen, Google only wants to show web pages that will display properly on such devices.

Where Do All of These Updates Leave Us?

Today, optimizing for specific keyword phrases has not just become difficult because of Panda & Penguin. It has now become less effective in driving traffic if those phrases do not match the *intent* of the searcher who is typing into Google.

Out of all the aforementioned Google updates, the one that had the big influence on my own SEO was Penguin. Google sent their Penguin into places that no SEO professional ever imagined they would dare to send it. Many will remember April 24, 2012, as the day the world of SEO changed forever. It was also the day that inspired me to release the first edition of this book, entitled **"SEO 2012 & Beyond - SEO will never be the same again"**. Google created such a major shift in the way they analyzed webpages that I now think in terms of Pre-Penguin and Post-Penguin SEO, and that will likely come across in this book.

SEO Today

Today, SEO is very different from even a couple of years ago. Google have put a number of measures in place to combat the manipulative actions of webmasters.

Ask a bunch of webmasters to define the term SEO and I bet you'll get a lot of different answers. Definitions will vary depending on the type of person you ask, and even when you ask them. SEO before Google introduced the Panda update was easy. After the Panda update, it was still relatively easy, but you needed to make sure your content was good. After Google released the Penguin update, SEO suddenly became a whole lot harder.

In 2015, phrases you'll hear being used by SEO experts will include:

1. On-page SEO
2. Off-page SEO
3. Link building
4. White hat SEO
5. Grey hat SEO
6. Black hat SEO

We've looked briefly at the first three of these, so let's quickly define the last three using a diagram.

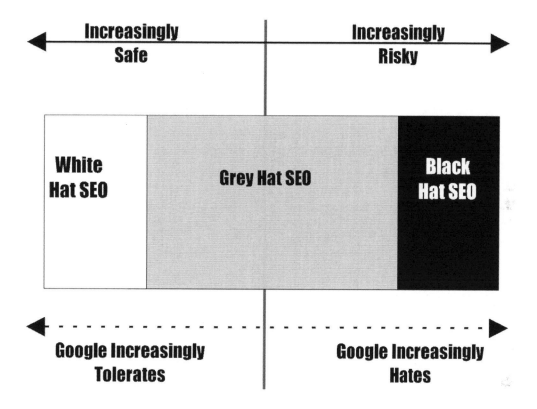

In the diagram above, you can see that we have three forms of SEO:

6. **White Hat SEO** – approved strategies for getting your page to rank well. Google offers guidelines to webmasters which spell out approved SEO strategies.

7. **Black Hat SEO** – these are the "loopholes" that Google are actively seeking out and penalizing for. They include a whole range of strategies from on-page keyword stuffing to backlink blasts using software to generate tens of thousands of backlinks to a webpage.

8. **Grey Hat SEO** – Strategies that lie between the two extremes. These are strategies that Google do not approve of, but are less likely to get your site penalized than black hat SEO. Grey hat tactics are certainly riskier than white hat SEO, but not as risky as black hat.

If you think of this as a sliding scale from totally safe "White Hat" SEO to totally dangerous "Black Hat" SEO, then you can imagine that as you move to the right with your SEO, you are more likely to get yourself into hot water with Google (at least in the long term). As you move more to the left with your SEO, you are more likely to be safer with Google. Google's tolerance level is somewhere in the grey hat area.

Staying somewhere in the middle may give you better returns for your time, but you do risk a penalty eventually.

Before Panda & Penguin, most webmasters knew where these lines were drawn and took their risks accordingly.

When Google introduced Panda, the only real change was that webmasters needed to make sure their website content was unique, interesting to visitors, and added something that no other webpage on the same topic provided. No small task, but to beat Panda, the goal was to create excellent content.

When Google introduced Penguin, they completely changed the face of SEO, probably forever, or at least for as long as Google continues to be the dominant search engine (which probably amounts to the same thing). Here is a diagrammatic representation of how SEO changed:

Post Penguin & Panda

	Increasingly Risky
White Hat SEO	Grey Hat SEO

Black Hat SEO

Google Approved Strategies

Increasing chance of a penalty

Google Tolerance

We've still got the safe "White Hat" SEO and unsafe "Black Hat". What's really changed is the "Grey Hat" SEO. Whereas previously it was reasonably safe, it's now become a lot riskier.

The "increasingly risky, increasingly safe" vertical divider that I drew in the centre of the first diagram (pre-Panda & Penguin) has now moved further to the left. In fact, it is right up against the edge of the white hat SEO.

You will notice that there is a new "Google Tolerance" line drawn on the diagram. This tolerance line can move from left to right at any time, depending on how Google tweak their algorithm. If they want to come down hard on "spammers", they'll move the line more to the left. If too many good sites get taken out as "collateral damage", as they call it, then they may move the tolerance line over to the right a bit (see the section later on "Trust Vs No-Trust"). Generally though, for all new sites and most others, the tolerance level is very close to the White Hat boundary, and this is what you need to be mindful of.

Webmasters who uses techniques which are further to the right of this tolerance line risk losing their rankings.

Although these diagrams are good to work from, they do not display the whole truth.

Let's just consider how trust changes the equation.

Trust Vs No-trust

The Google Tolerance Line will slide left or right depending on the site that is being ranked. For a site that has proven its worth, meaning Google trusts it a lot; we might see the diagram look like this:

A "Trusted" Site

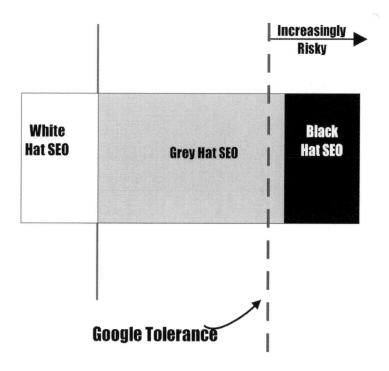

Yet for a new site, or one that has no track record to speak of, the diagram will probably look a lot more like this.

A "Non-trusted" Site

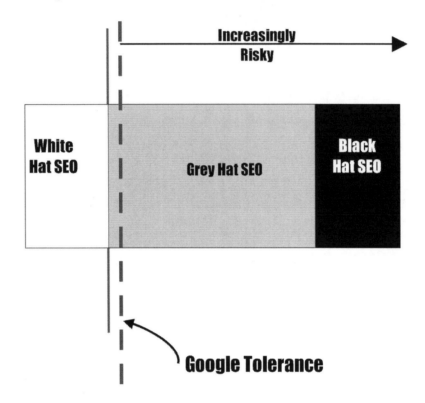

The only difference here is in the location of the "tolerance line".

In other words, Google are a lot more tolerant of sites which have built up authority and trust than they are of new sites, or sites which have not been able to attain a decent level of authority or trust.

A high authority site with lots of trust can withstand a certain amount of spammy SEO without incurring a penalty (see later when we discuss "negative SEO"). In other words, the more authority the site has, the more it can endure, or get away with.

A new site, on the other hand, would be quickly penalized for even a small amount of spammy SEO.

Webmasters Living in the Past

A lot of webmasters (or SEO companies vying for your business) may disagree with my take on modern-day SEO, and that's fine. The more people there are who just don't get it, the less competition there is for me and my clients.

I am sure you can still find people who will say this is all rubbish and that they can get your pages ranked for your search terms (depending on the severity of competition of course) by heavily back-linking the page using keyword rich anchor text.

The process they'll describe is eerily similar to the process I told you about in the section "How we used to rank pages", i.e. before 2010. It goes something like this:

1. Keyword research to find high demand, low competition phrases.

2. Create a page that is optimized for that keyword phrase.

3. Get lots of backlinks using that keyword phrase as anchor-text (the clickable text in a hyperlink).

4. Watch your page rise up the SERPs.

If you don't care about your business, then follow that strategy or hire someone to do it for you. You might get short term gains, but you'll run the risk of losing all your rankings further down the line when Google catches up with you (and catch up it will... probably sooner rather than later).

To lose all of your rankings on Google does not take a human review, though Google does use human reviewers on some occasions. No, getting your site penalised is much quicker and less hassle than that of human intervention. The process Google created for this is far more "automated" since the introduction of Panda and Penguin. Go over the threshold levels of what is acceptable, and the penalty is algorithmically determined and applied.

The good news is that algorithmic penalties can just as easily be lifted by removing the offending SEO and cleaning up your site. However, if that offending SEO includes low quality backlinks to your site (especially to the homepage), things become a little trickier.

Remember the SEO expert you hired that threw tens of thousands of backlinks at your site using his secret software? How can you get those backlinks removed? In most cases it's not easy, although Google do provide a "Disavow" tool that can help in a lot of instances. I'll tell you more about that later in the book. In extreme circumstances, moving the site to a brand new domain and starting afresh may be the only option.

In the rest of this book, I want to focus on what you need to do to help your pages rank better. I will be looking mainly at white-hat strategies, though I will venture a little into grey hat SEO as well. I won't be covering black-hat SEO at all though. This is because it's just not a long-term strategy. Remember, with the flick of a switch, Google can, and sometimes does, move the goal posts, leaving you out in the cold. Is it worth risking your long-term business plans for short-term gains?

OK, let's now get started with the four pillars of post-Penguin SEO.

The Four Pillars of Post-Penguin SEO

I have been doing SEO for over 10 years now and have always concentrated on long-term strategies. That's not to say I haven't dabbled in black hat SEO because I have, a little. Over the years, I have done a lot of experiments on all kinds of ranking factors. However, and without exception, *all* of the sites I promoted with black hat SEO have been penalized; every single one of them.

In this book, I don't want to talk about the murkier SEO strategies that will eventually cause you problems, so I'll concentrate on the safer techniques of white hat SEO.

I have divide SEO into four main pillars. These are:

1. Quality content
2. Site organization
3. Authority
4. What's in it for the visitor?

These are the four areas where you need to concentrate your efforts, so let's now have a look at each of them in turn.

1. Quality Content

Before we begin, let me just say that a lot of SEO "experts" have disagreed with me on the need for quality content as a major ranking factor. They will often cite exceptions in the search engines where pages rank well for competitive terms without much on-page content or with content of very little value. The fact that these exceptions rarely last more than a week or two eludes them.

Remember, bounce rates and time spent on a site are indicators to Google of whether a page gives a visitor what they want, or not. Poor content cannot hide in the Google top 10. Search engine users essentially vote out content that falls short on quality. They do this by their actions, or inactions, as the case may be. They vote by the length of time they stay on any particular site or page, and whether or not they visit any other pages while on that site (the latter examining overall site reputation). Additionally, Google also looks at what they do once they hit the back button and return to the SERPs.

If you are one of those people who question the need for quality content, then I encourage you to watch a video I recorded before you read the rest of this book. You can view it here:

http://ezseonews.com/lsivid
It's quite an eye opener.

What Google Tells Us About Quality Content

Google's Webmaster Guidelines offer advice to webmasters. They tell us what Google considers "good content", and what they consider as spam. Let's take a quick look at what the guidelines say about website content.

1. Create a useful, information-rich site

This one should be obvious. Create content that your visitors *want* to see.

2. Think about the words people use to search

...and try to incorporate them into your pages.

This particular guideline is one that I think will soon disappear. The reason I think this is because it's an open invitation for webmasters to fill their pages with keywords and phrases. Focusing on keywords usually results in a web page optimized for the search engines at the expense of the visitor's experience. Google openly labels that type of page as Webspam.

I actually think this guideline is probably remaining from the pre-Panda days. The best advice (which you will understand if you watched the video earlier in this chapter) is to think about the words people use to search, the synonyms of those words, and the searcher's intent. Questions you will want to ask include: what is the searcher looking for exactly? What words, phrases and topics does my page need to satisfy that intent?

We will look at all of this in more detail later in the book.

3. Try to use text instead of images for important names, content or links

Google's crawler does not recognize text in images, so if there is an important word or phrase that you need Google to know exists in any part of your page, use text instead. If it has to be an image for whatever reason, then use the ALT tag to create a description of the image which includes that phrase.

A great example of using text instead of images is in links on your site. Links are the most important factor in SEO, so the more the search engines know about the nature of a link the better. If you are linking to a page on your site about "purple furbies", then use **purple furbies** as the link text. This will tell Google that you (the webmaster) know the page you are linking to looks at purple furbies. These internal links also help rank a page for a specific term. Internal links are a safer way to get keyword rich anchor text into a link (something that is not so safe coming from other websites). You will see more about this in the section on "back-linking" later in the book.

4. Make <title> and ALT attributes descriptive

The <title> tag of your page is one of the most important areas in terms of SEO. Try to get your most important keyword(s) in there, but do not stuff keywords into the title. The title tag has two main objectives; one is to entice the searcher to click through from the search engines, and the other is to tell Google what your page is all about.

We talked about click through rates (CTR) earlier in the book, and looked at how important a factor they are in modern SEO. If you find that a page has a low CTR (something you can check in Google webmaster tools), then tweak the title to see if you can make it more enticing to searchers, and then monitor the CTR of the page in the coming days and weeks. Just know that better titles (ones that match the searcher's intent) will attract more clicks in the Google SERPs.

We talked about click through rates (CTR) earlier in the book, and looked at how important a factor they are in modern SEO. If you find a page has a low CTR (something you can check in Google webmaster tools), then tweak the title to see if you can make it more enticing to searchers. You then need to monitor the CTR of the page in the coming days and weeks. Just know that better titles (ones that match the searcher's intent) will attract more clicks in the Google SERPs than ones that don't.

NOTE: A page listed in the search results also contains a short description under its title. Google sometimes uses the text from the Meta Description tag of your web page for this. The description is typically a 160-character snippet used to summarize a web page's content. Search engines like Google may use these text snippets in the search results as a way to let visitors know what your page is about. You can do the same tweaking of the Meta Description tag as you do with the title tag to help increase CTR. However, this is less of an exact science since Google will sometimes grab text extracts from elsewhere on the page for the listing's description.

Let's now look at ALT tags. These are there for a very specific purpose. Their primary objective is to help people who have images turned off, for example, people with impaired vision. Often they will use text-to-voice software to read pages, so your ALT tags should help them with this. An ALT tag should describe the image to those users in a concise way. It is also a great place to insert a keyword phrase or synonym, but NEVER use ALT tags just as a place to stuff keywords.

5. Make pages for users, not search engines

This is probably the most important point in all of the Webmaster guidelines. If you keep this in mind at all times, then you'll be on the right path.

In the past, many webmasters created pages to please the search engines. They gave little or no thought to providing a good visitor experience. At least this was the case with those more interested in making money online than sharing valuable information on a given topic. Well, that was then and this is now.

Whatever you do in 2015 and beyond, don't just create content for the search engines in the hope of ranking better and building more traffic. Pleasing algorithms over people is an old hat tactic that no longer works. Instead, you need to create the content that your audience wants to see, read and interact with. Keeping your visitors happy makes Google happy. When you get to please the search engine giant, your authority and traffic will build in a safe, natural, and more sustainable way.

6. Avoid tricks designed to manipulate your rankings

Google offer you a rule of thumb. If you are comfortable explaining what you are doing to a Google employee, or one of your competitors (who could report you to Google), then you are probably doing things the right way. Another great test is to ask yourself whether you would do what you are doing if search engines didn't exist.

7. Make your website stand out in your field

No matter what niche you are in, and no matter what keywords you want to rank for, you ultimately have 10 other pages competing with you. They are the 10 web pages at the top of the Google SERPs. That's where you want to rank, right? Therefore, you need to ignore all the other tens of thousands of pages ranking on page two and beyond. Your focus is only on the top 10 slots of page one.

The questions you need to be ever mindful of are: How can I make my page stand out from these competitors? And, how can I make my page better, more engaging, different and valuable?

Google needs to see that your page adds to the top 10 in a unique way, and not merely blends in with the rest. In other words, you want to rise above being just another rehashed page on the same topic.

Google Tells Us to Avoid the Following

1. Automatically Generated Content

In an effort to build websites faster, webmasters have created a variety of tools, including some that can actually create content for you. Any content attained like this is very poor in quality and considered spam by Google. You should avoid any tool or service that offers to auto-generate content at all costs. This will get your site penalized or even completely de-indexed (removed from Google's SERPs).

Some webmasters go as far as having all the content on all their web pages automatically generated (and updated) from stuff on other websites. For example, they can use various data feeds (databases that contain information like product listings, and articles, etc.), and RSS feeds. This way they get to populate their web pages effortlessly, but their site has no unique or original content of its own. As these feeds update, so too do the pages on the site that has stolen the content.

The only time when using data feeds is a good idea is if you own the feed. This means its contents will be unique to your own site. An example would be an e-commerce site using a product feed.

2. Creating Pages with Little or No Original Content

Great content is King, and that means it has to be unique as well as well written. The term "thin page" describes content on a website that has little or no original material. These are pages which don't offer much value to the visitor. They include pages with very little written content (word count), or pages that might have a lot of content but it's not original. Being original is also more than just having a unique article that passes a Copyscape check (Copyscape is a free plagiarism tool that lets you check articles for uniqueness). Truly original content also means offering new ideas, thoughts and insights, things not found on the other pages in the top 10.

3. Hidden Text

In an effort to rank for more search terms, some webmasters make text snippets on their web pages invisible. This typically includes keyword rich text using lots of related terms the webmaster hopes to rank for. It's not hard to make text invisible to the visitor. All you have to do is use the same colour font as the page background, i.e. white text on a white background. However, if you try to hide text from Google in this way, well, you're on a hiding to nothing to be frank. This used to work several years ago, but today it will more than likely get your site penalised.

Hidden links also come under the umbrella of hidden text. This was a tactic used in the past to spread link juice around, maybe by linking a full stop (period) to another page in an effort to make it rank better.

There are a number of other ways to hide text on a web page, but Google are on to all of them, so my advice to you is don't do it.

4. Doorway Pages

This term refers to pages that are set up to rank for a single specific keyword phrase. They are highly optimized for that phrase, and their sole purpose is to rank high for the chosen search term. Traffic is then typically (though not always) funnelled to another page or site from the doorway page.

5. Scraped Content

Scraped content is the content copied from other websites. Spammers often do this to add more material to their own websites, quickly and with very little effort.

Scraping can involve grabbing entire articles or just parts of another webpage. Scraping tactics also include copying someone else's content and then swapping out synonyms in an attempt to make the stolen content appear unique.

Even pages that embed podcasts or other shared media like YouTube videos, for example, can be considered scraped content unless the webmaster adds their own unique commentary or thoughts to the page that embeds the media. A webpage should offer value to a visitor, and that includes a unique experience.

6. Participating in Affiliate Programs Without Adding Sufficient Value

One of Google's recent algorithm changes targeted web pages that were heavy on adverts. Google reasons that too many ads on a page make for a bad user experience. Therefore, ads should be secondary to the main content, and must not dominate the page.

Another thing you need to be aware of is how to properly run reviews sites, if that's your thing. Your reviews need to be totally unique and contain original thoughts and ideas. Your reviews must also contain information that is not available on the merchant site, or other affiliate sites.

If you simply go to Amazon and use their product description and user comments, then your page is not only scraped content, but it also fails to add sufficient value. Reviews need to have original thoughts, ideas and suggestions to be of any importance. After all, why would someone want to read your reviews when they can read all the exact same information on Amazon or the manufacturer's own site?

A good test is to strip out all of the adverts and scraped content from a page (even if you re-wrote it in your own words), and then see whether the page still offers sufficient value to the visitor.

7. Loading Pages with Keywords

In an effort to rank for more search terms, some webmasters stuff additional keywords into their page. Quite often, you will see a list of keywords on the page, maybe in the form of a "related terms" section, or a list of US states, as two examples.

Another way to overload a web page with keywords is when the author reuses keywords or key phrases too many times (keyword density) in the content. High keyword density is another old hat practice that no longer works.

Keyword density is the percentage of times a keyword or key phrase appears on a web page compared to the total number of words on that same page. When the same keywords or key phrases get too much use, the sentence reads unnaturally or grammatically incorrect. This wasn't such an issue when webmasters used to write for search engines over their visitors.

Google offer this example as an explanation:

"We sell **custom cigar humidors**. Our **custom cigar humidors** are handmade. If you're thinking of buying a **custom cigar humidor**, please contact our **custom cigar humidor** specialists at **custom.cigar.humidors**@example.com."

As you can see, that is totally unnatural and not easy to read, yet this is exactly the sort of trash that used to dominate the SERPs of yesteryear.

Stuffing pages with keywords is clearly something that is for the benefit of the search engines. Try it and you page/site will get a slap from Google. Like so many other such tactics, this used to work once, but not anymore.

8. User-generated SPAM

A good example of user-generated spam includes the comments posted on your site. If you accept comments, and you should do by the way, make sure you moderate them. In addition, only accept legitimate comments that add to the "conversation" you started on the page. Never approve comments that simply attempt to stroke your ego with things like "Great blog", or comments that ask totally irrelevant questions like, "Hey, great WordPress theme, what is it?" Only approve comments that raise legitimate points, or ask legitimate questions about your article specifically. Trash anything that's non-specific, or mark it as SPAM if it's obvious.

Another type of user-generated content that you need to be careful of is guest posts. If you accept articles from other people and post them on your site, you must never accept any content that is below your own standards. I would also suggest you never allow others to place external links in the body of an article. If the author wants to include a link back to their website, only allow it in the author's bio section at the end of the article. Furthermore, make sure those links are nofollow. When I have suggested this in the past, people have complained that if they follow my guidelines, they won't get people to write guest posts because there is nothing in it for the writer. Well, my reply is this: if they don't follow these guidelines, then they won't have a site to accept guest posts. If your site reaches authority status in your niche, then writers will benefit from the exposure; something they would not have otherwise received. And anyway, having their article and name published on a well-known and well-respected website or blog is of more value to them than some link in an author's bio box.

A Summary - Quality Content & an Example

There are a number of different types of content that you can add to your website. This includes articles, product reviews, quizzes, videos, etc. However, no matter what type of content you are looking at, it has to adhere to the following three points:

1. Create for the visitor, not the search engines. That means it needs to read well and have no visible signs of keyword stuffing.

2. Add value to the top 10 SERP (if you want to rank in the top 10, your page has to be seen as adding something unique to that collection of pages).

3. Give your visitors what they want. Create the content they want to see.

To put it simply, all of the content on your site has to be the best that you can make it.

A good rule of thumb, as suggested by Google, is this: would your content look out of place published in a glossy magazine?

If you ever hire ghost-writers, be sure to proofread their content first to make sure that any **facts are correct** and there are **no spelling or grammatical errors**.

As you read through the content that you intend to publish on your website, ask yourself these questions:

- Is it content that your visitors will find really useful?
- Is there information in there that your visitors are unlikely to know, and therefore find informative?
- If it's a review, does it sound overly hyped up? Are both sides of the argument covered, i.e. positives and negatives? Is there information in the review that is not available on the manufacturer's website or other affiliate sites? Does the review offer a different way of looking at things which may help the buyer make a better informed decision prior to purchase?

OK, so we know what Google does want. Now let's take a look at some poor content, just so that we can identify what won't work.

Here is the first paragraph of an article I found online a few years ago. I'm sure you can guess what the author was trying to optimize the page for.

Understanding Pomegranate Juice Benefits

Some people may not be that knowledgeable about pomegranate juice benefits but it is actually a very effective source of Vitamin C. The pomegranate fruit contains a lot of healthy nutrients and you can get a lot of good immune system boosters out of pomegranate juice benefits. It can actually provide around 16% of the required amount of Vitamin C that adults need to take on a daily basis. Pomegranate juice benefits also include Vitamin B5 as well as the antioxidant element of polyphenols and potassium.

You won't find this page in Google search anymore, and it doesn't take a rocket scientist to figure out why ;)

It's not too difficult to guess the main phrase the author was targeting, is it. In fact, it reminds me of the Google "do not do" example we saw earlier about custom cigar humidors.

"Pomegranate juice benefits" sticks out like a sore thumb. In fact, in a relatively short article (just 415 words) that phrase appeared 17 times. That's a key phrase density of 4%.

How many people think a key phrase density of 4% is OK or natural? Is repeating the same phrase so many times in one piece normal? Yet even 4% was moderate in the heyday of trash articles.

Do you want to know what a natural density is?

Natural density of a keyword phrase is whatever density occurs naturally when an expert in their field writes an article.

If you look back at that pomegranate paragraph, there is an even bigger sin.

This sentence does not make sense:

*"The pomegranate fruit contains a lot of healthy nutrients and you can get a lot of good immune system boosters out of **pomegranate juice benefits**."*

It doesn't make sense at all. It should finish with "...out of pomegranate juice", but the webmasters used it as an opportunity to stuff in that main key phrase again, making the sentence read nonsense.

This is a very clear indicator that the author was stuffing that phrase into the article in an attempt to help it rank higher for that phrase.

The sad thing is that this type of article may well have ranked well before Panda and Penguin came along. Why is that sad? Because web searchers had to put up with this kind of rubbish constantly. It's not the kind of stuff they were searching for, but it was often the kind of stuff they got nonetheless.

Today, no amount of sneaky black hat techniques could get this page into the top 10, at least not for the long term. That is the difference between pre and post Panda/Penguin SEO. It's the reason this page no longer exists in Google, or in fact online. The webmaster has closed the site down, presumably after it stopped being profitable.

If I do a Google search for **pomegranate juice benefits**, the top ranked page (at the time of writing) does NOT include the exact phrase at all! How's that for a natural density? The number two ranked site includes it once in 2,696 words (a density of just 0.04%), and the number three ranked page does not include the term at all.

The lesson to learn from this is to throw keyword density rules out of the window.

What may be a surprise to many, is that out of the top 10 pages ranking for the term "pomegranate juice benefits", only ONE has that phrase in the page title. In fact, **only**

one of the top 10 pages includes that exact phrase anywhere in the article.

Maybe you think that statistic is just a fluke, so try it for yourself. Enter any search term that isn't a brand name or product name. You will see that, in general, the top 10 search results in Google list far fewer pages containing the actual search term. This number has decreased over the last year (since I last updated this book).

Okay, so the question is this: how is Google able to decide how to rank webpages for the term "pomegranate juice benefits", or any other search term, if they are not looking for that actual phrase in the content?

The answer lies with the words on the page, but in a less obvious, though totally natural way.

Let me ask you a question.

Does Your Article Sound as If an Expert Wrote It?

The reason I ask is because when somebody who really knows their subject writes an article, they will use a certain "niche vocabulary". That is, they will use words and phrases that actually define the topic of the article very well.

You can read an article I wrote about this over three years ago called: "Niche Vocabulary - why poor content can't hide in Google".

http://famousbloggers.net/niche-vocabulary-poor-content-google.html

You will see in that article, that if the content does not contain its niche vocabulary, then it's unlikely to rank well in Google, even when it includes the actual target key phrase.

Every Article You Write Will Have Its Own Niche Vocabulary

Articles on related topics may well use a lot of the same niche vocabulary, but they will also contain other words and phrases that define the topic more specifically.

Let's look at an example of this.

To carry out a test, I found a number of words in the top 10 pages of Google ranking for the term epilepsy. These words appeared on many of the top 10 pages ranking for that term. These are what I call theme words (or niche vocabulary), i.e. words that commonly appear in articles written on a given topic.

Here are the theme words I found for the term epilepsy:

Age, aid, anti, brain, cause, children, control, develop, diagnosis, diet, doctor, drugs, epilepsy, epileptic, guide, health, help, home, information, ketogenic, life, living, log, medical, medications, part, plan, research, seizure, seizure-free, seizures, side, special, support, surgery, symptoms, take, term, test, time, treatment, types, unit, and work.

I then chose two sub-niches in the epilepsy fields to see if these words appeared on those pages as well. These sub niches were:

1. Epilepsy treatment

2. Ketogenic diet

Both of these terms are highly related to epilepsy. Just for reference, the ketogenic diet is a high-fat, adequate-protein, low-carbohydrate diet used primarily to treat difficult-to-control epilepsy, mostly in young patients. Since both of these terms talk about epilepsy, they both should contain a lot of the epilepsy niche vocabulary.

First let's have a look at the top ranking pages for the term **epilepsy**. Here is a screenshot showing the number one ranked article with the theme words that I found earlier highlighted in the text:

You can only see a small section of the article here as it's quite long. Even so, I'm sure you will agree that the theme words used are obvious throughout the piece.

Let's repeat this, but this time using the number one ranked article for the term **epilepsy treatment**:

with the introduction of dilantin (warner-lambert), has been a triumph of mode
e. the development of newer medications, especially tegretol (ciba-geigy) a
eckitt & colman) has meant that epilepsy can be suppressed in most patients
serious or annoying side effects. this is not to say that every patient can be full
led, or that side effects do not occur. a continuing effort is being made by
onal pharmaceutical companies to find safer, more effective treatment
y. new drugs are not cascading onto the market however, for the high cost of
h, development and marketing (about a$150 million for any new drug) is an
nt disincentive. how do drugs prevent seizures? strange to say, most of the
sed in treating epilepsy today were discovered to have anti-epileptic proper
ce. we have used these drugs with great benefit for years without really know
y work. however, a more systematic search for new antiepileptic s is r
ay, based on research progress in understanding how neurones transmit
s to each other, and our increasing knowledge of the structure and function of
ne which surrounds each neurone. the messages that one neurone sends to th
ditated by releasing neurotransmitter chemicals, can either excite the neurone
ine, or can inhibit its electrical activity. the identification of gamaa-amino butyri

Once again, we see the theme words sprinkled throughout the content, as we would expect, since this article is also about epilepsy.

Let's now look at the final example, which is the **ketogenic diet**:

ketogenic diet was then gradually forgotten as new anticonvulsant medications
developed. the ketogenic diet has recently been 'rediscovered' and is achieving
increasingly widespread use. its modern day role as alternative management for c
with difficult-to-control epilepsy is currently being re-defined. the ketogenic di
a 'fad' or a 'quack diet', but rather is an alternative medical treatment child
difficult-to-control epilepsy. the ketogenic diet should only be used under the
supervision of a physician and a dietician. background fasting to achieve control
seizure was described in both the bible and during the middle ages, but it was c
during the early 1920s that scientific papers first appeared describing the benefici
effects of prolonged fasting for children whose epilepsy could not be controlled
few medications then available. these papers claimed that starvation, drinking on
for 10 to 20 or more days, could result in control seizure for prolonged peri
time. during this era, when the metabolic effects of diabetes were also being stud
was noted that the biochemical effects of fasting could be mimicked by eating a d

This too has the same theme words for epilepsy sprinkled throughout its content.

Since all of these articles have epilepsy "theme words" sprinkled within them, they could all theoretically rank for the term epilepsy. Google will know these articles are about epilepsy because they contain epilepsy-related words and phrases.

In addition to the core set of epilepsy-related theme words, each of these articles also contain **a slightly different set of theme words** which help to define what area of epilepsy they are discussing. We could show this by finding theme words specific to each of the three articles. We would see words and phrases with a different emphasis popping up (though there would still be a core of epilepsy related words).

To illustrate this further, I found a number of "theme phrases" - 2, 3 and 4-word phrases that are common to the top 10 ranked pages for the three terms – epilepsy, epilepsy treatment, and ketogenic diet.

Here is a table of the results, showing the theme words and phrases appearing in the top 10 pages ranked for each of the search terms:

Epilepsy	Epilepsy Treatment	Ketogenic Diet
activity in the brain atkins diet blood sugar causes of epilepsy epilepsy medication epilepsy medications epilepsy surgery ketogenic diet part of the brain seizure medicines temporal lobe vagus nerve	adverse effects aid for seizures anticonvulsant drug anticonvulsant drugs anti-epileptic drug anti-epileptic medications anti-seizure medications controlling seizures epileptic control epileptic seizures ketogenic diet seizure control seizure medications temporal lobe treatment of epilepsy treatments for epilepsy	anticonvulsant drug anticonvulsant drugs beta hydroxybutyric acid body fat control of seizures control seizures diet controls seizures different anticonvulsants high fat high fat diet high fat intake medical treatment for children protein and carbohydrate seizure control seizure type treatment of seizure while on the diet

This table clearly shows that each of the three search terms has a different niche vocabulary.

All three articles have theme words relating to epilepsy, as we would expect. However, each of the articles also has their own set of theme phrases which help to distinguish the actual sub-niche within epilepsy.

1. The **epilepsy** article has a wide range of theme phrases relating to all aspects of epilepsy.

2. The **epilepsy treatment** article focused more on phrases related to the treatment of epilepsy (no big surprise there).

3. The **ketogenic diet** article had more theme phrases relating to the diet itself and the control of seizures.

Anyone who read earlier versions of this book will recognise the Epilepsy example from those editions.   Therefore, the example is a few years old and you may question whether the information is still valid today.   For that reason, let's do a brand new example to check.

I ran an analysis of the top 10 pages ranking in Google for the term "Health benefits of Krill Oil".   By the way, at the time of writing, not one page listed in the top 10 search results had that exact phrase in the title.

Here are the theme words I found on seven or more of the top 10 pages:

Acids, age, animal, balance, benefits, better, blood, capsules, cardiovascular, care, cell, cholesterol, clinical, daily, dha, diet, disease, eat, effects, epa, fatty, fish, flu, food, health, healthy, heart, human, krill, levels, liver, lower, nutrition, oil, omega-3, protein, ratio, red, reduce, research, safe, side, skin, source, sources, studies, study, supplement, supplements, test, and women.

There are 51 words in that list and all 51 show on seven or more of the top 10 pages that rank for the term "health benefits of krill oil".

I also checked for 2, 3 and 4-word phrases found on the same top 10 pages. Here are the ones I found:

Allergic reaction, amino acid, bad cholesterol, benefits of krill, benefits of krill oil, brain health, cardiovascular disease, cell membranes, cholesterol levels, clinical studies, clinical study, cod liver, crp levels, daily dose, dietary supplement, effects of krill oil, experimental animal, eye health, fatty acids, fish oil, fish oil supplement, fish oil supplements, fish oils, food source, free radicals, health benefits, health care, health food, healthy cholesterol, heart disease, heart health, krill oil, krill oil arthritis benefits, krill oil benefit, krill oil daily, krill protein, lose weight, metabolic syndrome, nitric oxide, oil supplement, omega 3, omega-3 fatty acids, omega-3 phospholipid, omega-3 polyunsaturated fatty acids, pain killer, polyunsaturated fatty acids, premenstrual syndrome, rheumatoid arthritis, side effects, source of omega-3, sources of omega-3, triglyceride levels, and weight loss.

The Difference Between Theme Words and Theme Phrases in My Analysis

The difference between theme words and theme phrases is obvious.   Theme words contain just one word, whereas theme phrases contain more than one word.

When it comes to Google, finding theme phrases in an article is further confirmation of a theme, but when I am analysing top ranking pages, I concentrate on the theme words, not the phrases.   Why?   Because theme phrases often have several variations which essentially mean the same thing, and ARE the same thing to Google.   An example in the list above would include:

- fish oil supplement
- fish oil supplements

Both mean the same thing, and just because an article contains one and not the other, that does not make one piece any more or less important.

A much better strategy would be to place the importance on the words that make up those phrases (fish, oil and supplement(s)).

Here is another example:

- omega 3
- omega-3 fatty acids
- omega-3 phospholipid
- omega-3 polyunsaturated fatty acids

Just because an article on krill oil does not specifically use the phrase **omega-3 polyunsaturated fatty acids,** does not mean it hasn't talked about omega-3.

If I concentrate on the words: **omega-3, fatty, acids, phospholipid and polyunsaturated** in my analysis, then I can cover all variations of these phrases.

I hope you can see that there is not much point counting individual theme phrases. The important theme phrases comprise all of the important theme words, so this is what I concentrate on when writing authoritative articles.

OK, let's get back to the experiment.

I wanted to see how many of my 51 theme words were being used by pages ranked in the top 100 of Google.

For this analysis, I grouped pages ranking in the following positions:

1-10, 11-20, 21-30, 31-40, 41-50 & 51-60

I wanted to see how well the pages in these positions were themed for my 51 keywords. I analysed each page individually, and then averaged the results out for the group.

Here are those results:

Position 1-10, on average, used 86% of my theme words.

Position 11-20, on average, used 81% of my theme words.

Position 21-30, on average, used 78% of my theme words.

Position 31-40, on average, used 69% of my theme words.

Position 41-50, on average, used 69% of my theme words.

Position 51-60, on average, used 73% of my theme words.

As you can see, all of the pages in the top 60 contained a good number of my theme words, with all pages averaging between 69%-86%.

Taking this a step further, I then wanted to see how well those pages ranked further down the SERPs were themed.

I grabbed the URLs ranking at:

100-109, 200-209 and 300-309

Position 100-109, on average, used 65% of my theme words.

Position 200-209, on average, used 72% of my theme words.

Position 300-309, on average, used 62% of my theme words.

So even those web pages ranked down in the 100–300 range are well-themed, containing a good proportion of my 51 theme words.

By the way, the reason I didn't analyse pages ranked lower than 300 is because Google doesn't actually include more than a few hundred URLs in their SERPs.

Colon Cleanse Capsules, Eye Supplements, Krill Oil and Acai Capsules.

> In order to show you the most relevant results, we have omitted some
> entries very similar to the 381 already displayed.
> If you like, you can repeat the search with the omitted results included.

Searches related to health benefits of krill oil

health benefits of krill oil **to the skin**	health benefits **flax seed** oil
health benefits of krill oil **supplements**	krill oil **supplements**
health benefits **yerba mate tea**	benefits of krill oil **pills**
health benefits **fish** oil	**mega red** krill oil benefits

‹ Goooogle

Previous   1 2 3 **4**

I did a Google search for **health benefits of krill oil**, showing 100 results per page. On page four, the results end with Google telling me that the rest of the pages in the index are similar to these first 381. Therefore, Google only ranks 381 pages for this phrase.

It's very interesting that all of the pages included in the SERPs seemed well themed around a core set of theme words, and we can harvest those theme words by analysing the top 10 results in Google for any given term.

Final Test in My Experiment

It's looking like all web pages ranked in Google for a search term are themed around a core set of keywords and phrases. Any page that does not cut the mustard doesn't appear in the main set of search results (the 381 pages we saw in the previous screen shot).

Because it's so important to know what Google wants with regards to "quality" content, I had the idea to test this still further. If all web pages really are themed around a group of related words, then I should be able to analyse the pages ranked 300-310 and grab the theme words from those pages, instead of the top 10. If I re-analyse the pages ranked in positions 1-10, 100-110, 200-210 & 300-310, I should find a similar high percentage of those theme words used in each case.

OK, here's what I did.

I extracted the theme words from the pages ranked 300-310 using Web Content Studio (my own tool that helps webmasters to write better, quality, themed content in a way that mimics natural writers). I then refined the selection, only accepting theme words that appeared on seven or more of those 10 pages. I ended up with the following list of 49 theme words:

Acid, acids, antarctic, anti-inflammatory, antioxidant, antioxidants, astaxanthin, benefits, blood, body, brain, cholesterol, damage, deficiency, dha, disease, effects, epa, essential, fat, fatty, fish, food, health, healthy, heart, high, inflammation, inflammatory, krill, levels, nutrition, oil, omega, omega-3, phospholipid, powerful, products, protein, rates, red, side, skin, source, supplement, supplements, support, vitamins, and weight.

I then checked these theme words against the pages ranked 1-10, 100-109, 200-209, and 300-309. The results were interesting:

Position 1-10, on average, used 77% of the theme words.

Position 100-109, on average, used 66% of the theme words.

Position 200-209, on average, used 69% of the theme words.

Position 300-309, on average, used 75% of the theme words.

OK, we expected a high percentage of the theme words in those pages ranked 300-309, because those are the pages that I used to collect the theme words. Those pages used an average of 75% of my theme words (remember I chose the words that only appeared on seven or more pages, so that percentage sounds about right).

However, look at the pages ranked 1-10. They actually used a higher percentage of theme words than the pages from which the theme words were collected. The top 10 pages used 77% of the theme words.

The pages ranked 100-109 and 200-209 where no slouches either. They used, on average, 66% and 69% of the theme words.

All of this goes to show that, on average, ALL of the web pages that rank in Google are well themed around a set of "niche vocabulary". That is quite exciting, but also a little scary. If ALL of the pages ranked in Google are well-themed, chances are they are all good quality. Based on this knowledge, how on earth do you beat them into the top 10? Well, that is where you need to give your visitors what they want by making your page "special". In other words, give them something extra, something not offered by the other pages in the top 10. Providing you do this well, you will make Google sit up and take notice of your content.

Before we leave these experiments, you might like to watch a video I created about Google and Latent Semantic Indexing (LSI):

http://ezseonews.com/lsivid2

How to Use This Information to Write Better Content

If you are an expert in the field you are writing about, you will automatically and naturally use the theme words and phrases as you write about the topic, and without having to think too much about it. The truth is that you need to include these theme words and phrases if your article is to adequately cover the topic.

If, however, you are not an expert, then things are a little more difficult. You need to find which words and phrases are important to the topic that you want to write about before you start writing.

As you write the content, the idea is to sprinkle in relevant theme words and include a small number of highly relevant theme phrases too. This will help the search engines identify the topic so much easier.

The theme phrases you use in a webpage should be the most important ones for that topic. These are the ones which will tell the search engines what that page is all about. Do not, under any circumstances, use theme words or phrases more often than is necessary. For example, don't repeat a phrase 3-4 times simply because you want that page to rank for that term. Google's Penguin will be straight onto you if you do, and that could see your rankings drop for keyword stuffing, or the unnatural use of keywords.

Below is an example of a badly written article where theme phrases have been repeated solely for the search engines. Ignoring the quality of the information in this piece, let's just look at an example of keyword stuffing:

DIY Architecture

Let's say you are planning a room addition. Did you know that you already possess the talents which allow you to calculate a comfortable size for the room addition? You may even possess some good design skills. Now you might think that I am wrong on this one.

For sake of discussion, let's assume that your local zoning ordinances will permit you to do just about anything. Some cities have strict setback lines and so forth that may limit the size of your planned addition - you must be aware of these limitations.

Go into your present living room. How does it feel? Imagine if it were say 6 feet wider and 8 feet longer. Maybe this size would allow you the space for that new couch, or a fireplace, built-in bookcases, whatever. The point is this. Use your existing rooms as starting points. You can measure them and stretch them to suit your needs. You need to start thinking in terms of space and how much you need.

Putting it on Paper

Remember earlier how I told you that my drafting skills were poor. Today, you don't need to know how to draw! If you have a fairly modern computer and sufficient memory, there are many affordable computer design programs that will draw your planned room addition.

I have highlighted one phrase that occurs three times, but I could have easily chosen a different example in this same article. The phrase is "room addition" and to me it sticks out because it is actually a little awkward to read, unnatural even, when you read the text around it (which is just fluff and padding anyway). This looks a lot like a doorway page designed to rank for a single high demand, high profit keyword.

Checking the Google Keyword Planner confirms this:

	Save all	Search terms (1)		
	Keyword	Competition	Global Monthly Searches ?	Approximate CPC (Search) ?
☐	room addition ▾	High	60,500	€2.67

That phrase has 60,500 monthly searches, and costs advertisers around 2.67 Euros PER CLICK.

The "room addition" webmaster used AdSense advertising on the page, and that is further confirmation to me that he was creating doorway pages. These types of pages exist for the search engines, and their only purpose is to rank well for single, high-profit keywords.

Funnily enough, the site that hosts this particular article used to be a site that Google showed off as a quality AdSense/Affiliate website. This was probably because of its spectacular earnings in the AdSense program. In spite of that, this site was later penalized during the initial rounds of Panda and Penguin; something which caused a lot of webmasters to conclude that Google does not like affiliate sites. After all, an affiliate site that the search engine giant once showcased as a shining example ended up getting a Google slap.

My view on this is that Google simply does not like poor or spammy content. This particular site was lucky to get away with its shabby articles for as long as it did, and most probably never got a real in-depth human review.

When Google introduced Panda and Penguin, automated quality checks became the norm. This meant that EVERY site could now be thoroughly checked for quality. These new checks obviously identified the page above, along with other pages on the same site, as low quality content, and therefore in violation of the Google guidelines. Looking through a lot of the earlier content on that site, I'd agree that it was penalized for good reason. If I were the webmaster of that site, my priority would have been to remove all the doorway pages and thin content from the site, knowing that if they remained in place, site penalties would continue.

Finding Theme Words & Phrases

You have a couple of options when it comes to finding theme words for your content.

Option 1 – Google SERPs + SEOQuake

The first option is 100% free and involves using the Google SERPs together with a browser plugin called SEOQuake (a program, which allows users to view a large number of SE parameters on the fly).

How to use:

1. Install SEO Quake in your browser. There are versions for Firefox, Opera, Safari

and Chrome.

2. Go to Google and search for the phrase you want to rank for.

3. Visit each of the top 10 pages in turn, and click the SEOQuake button to show the menu:

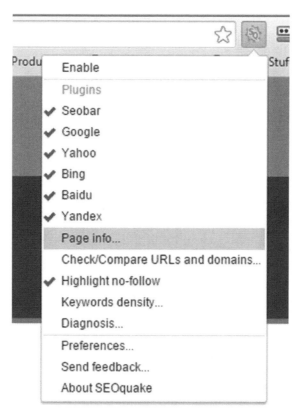

4. Select **Page Info** from that menu.

The resulting **page info** screen includes lists of keyword densities. We're not interested in the density itself. We want to know what that density tells us about the importance of the word or phrase.

Here is a density report for my **health benefits of krill oil** search phrase:

Keywords density:

Total number of words: 3709

Keyword	Found in	Repeats	Density
krill	T, D, K	68	1.83%
oil	T, D, K	65	1.75%
view		42	1.13%
webmd	T, D	32	0.86%
health		27	0.73%
abstract		27	0.73%
treatments		18	0.49%
fatty		18	0.49%
acids		16	0.43%
information	D, K	14	0.38%
vitamin		14	0.38%
omega-3		13	0.35%
medical	D, K	12	0.32%
blood		12	0.32%
fish		11	0.30%
healthy		10	0.27%

It should be no surprise that this top ranked page includes the words "krill", "oil" and "health" in the top five most used words on the page.

You'll also find 2, 3 and 4-word phrases listed lower down the report.

By going through each of the top 10 pages and checking which words and phrases appear the most times, you can then build up your list of theme words and phrases to include in your own content.

Option 2 – Web Content Studio (WCS)

I wrote a tool that I personally use called Web Content Studio (WCS). As it's my own tool, I do stand to profit from any sales from it, and therefore need to be upfront and transparent about that.

Since I do not want this book to be a sales pitch for my own products, I won't be going into details on how to use it. Instead, I'll just list the main benefits and offer you a URL where you can check it out for yourself.

The main benefits of using Web Content Studio are as follows:

1. The speed of finding niche vocabulary. Type in the phrase you want to rank for and WCS will return lists of words and phrases on the pages that rank in the top 10.

2. WCS will tell you how many of the top 10 pages each phrase appears on. This is important because a phrase that appears 100 times in the top 10 may appear 100 times on a single page, and not once on any of the other pages. The most important words appear on most of the top 10 pages, so these are the ones we need to target and these are the ones WCS delivers.

3. WCS has a WYSIWYG (What You See Is What You Ge) editor. This allows you to create your content within the program, and then run reports to check the theme and quality of your work.

OK, that's enough on WCS. If you want to see me using WCS to write an article, you can visit this page:

http://ezseonews.com/writing-content/how-i-write-a-top-quality-article/

For more details on the tool itself, visit:

http://webcontentstudio.com

We now know the importance of having niche vocabulary in our content, along with the ways to find it. That will go a long way to making sure the articles you write are quality. Once you get to understand the niche vocabulary in your chosen topic, you can then use it naturally as you compose your content.

There is a number of other on-page factors that you need to get right too, so let's take a look at those now.

On Page SEO Factors to Get Right

The Title Tag

The title tag is probably the most important ranking factor on your page in terms of SEO benefits. It is also vital in terms of persuading Google searchers to click on your link in the SERPs. In the *source code of your web page, the title tag looks like this:

<title>Title Goes Here</title>

* Source code is the basic backbone of most web pages (invisible, or under the hood so to speak). Source code includes a series of tags that instruct the internet browser software how to display the page as well as the actual page content that is visible to the viewer on the front end. Source code is also an essential factor with regards to SEO, as it allows search engine bots to better read your page and page elements.

Search engines look at the words in your title tag to determine what your page is about. Therefore, you should try to get your main keyword phrase into the title. The closer to the beginning of the title tag your keyword is, the better it will serve you.

If I was writing a web page about the health benefits of krill oil, the important phrases in that search terms are: krill oil and health benefits.

If I do a search on Google for **health benefits of krill oil,** here are the title tags of the top five pages ranking for that term.

Krill oil: Uses, Side Effects, Interactions and Warnings – WebMD

Krill Oil Benefits – Learn all the Wonderful Benefits of Krill Oil

Benefits of **Krill Oil** with Omega 3 Fats

Why **Krill Oil** Is Good for Your Heart | **Krill Oil Benefits**

Krill Oil: Benefits, Dangers & Side Effects - Drugs.com

All of these pages are from authority sites in the health niche, so they will have a massive ranking advantage over smaller sites. Anyway, the point is that you can still see they've included the main keywords in the title tag.

All five pages have the phrase **krill oil** near the beginning of the tag, and some duplicate that phrase at the end as well. Where possible, always try to get the most important words at or near to the beginning of the title tag.

The big omission in those titles is the word "health". Not one of those five pages includes that word in their title tag. However, all five of these sites are massive health authority sites, so Google can pretty much assume the benefits refer to health.

Only the first page in the ranking does not use either the word health or benefit(s), but that is WebMD. WebMD is an authority site that Google trusts for all health related searches. The way Google have evolved over recent years means it can now accurately determine a searcher's intent. If someone searches for health benefits of krill oil, Google will understand that they are looking for the kind of information provided by that #1 ranked WebMD article. WebMD have earned their reputation.

When creating your title tag, try to write one that not only includes the words that make up your main phrase or concept, but something that entices people to click your link when they read the title.

Keep your title tag to 67 **characters or less**. Any longer than that and it gets truncated in the search results.

Title tags on every page of your site should be unique. Never use the same title tag on two or more pages.

It is worth monitoring the click through rates (CTR) for your pages. If the CTR appears low, you can tweak the title tag to see if you can increase the CTR. The Title and Meta Description tags are the two variables you have the most control over in your quest for better CTR in the Google SERPs.

The Meta Description Tag

The Meta Description tag is not as important as the title tag, but you should still create a unique, interesting and enticing description on all of your pages nonetheless. Google will sometimes use the Meta Description tag in the search results, as the description of a listing, so it's worth creating a good one just in case.

In the source code of your web page, the Meta Description looks like this:

<meta name="description" content="Description goes here."/>

Here are the Meta Descriptions of the top five pages ranking in Google for the krill oil term we used earlier.

1. Find patient medical information for **krill oil** on WebMD including its uses, effectiveness, side effects and safety, interactions, user ratings and products that have it.

2. **Krill Oil** will protect your heart, lower your cholesterol, relieve PMS symptoms, fight aging and inflammation, optimize your brain's capabilities, and boost your overall **health**!

3. **Krill oil** is one of the best sources of omega 3 fats, which greatly influence your gene expression and overall **health**.

4. **Krill oil** supplementation helps reduce triglyceride levels in adults, lowering your risk of heart disease.

5. **Krill Oil** information from Drugs.com, includes **Krill Oil** side effects, interactions and indications.

As you can see, all five Meta Descriptions include the main keyword phrase **Krill Oil**. However, they don't use the words "health" or "benefits" as much as the page title. What you will see is other related words and phrases appearing, like **protect your heart, lower cholesterol, supplement/supplementation, risks, heart disease**, etc. These are some of the niche vocabulary for the search term, and it's a great idea to get some of the important vocabulary into the Meta Description (and title if you can fit it in).

When I write a Meta Description, I always create it at the same time as I do the title tag. I want them to complement each other. I will have a list of the most significant words and phrases in a hierarchy, with the most important ones at the top. Top of my list for this search term would be **krill oil** and **health benefits** (or just benefits if my site was a health site). Lower down my list would be phrases like **lower triglycerides**, **heart health,** and **side effects**, etc.

The most important phrase, in this case krill oil, would go into both tags. The Title would be written to include any other vital keywords related to the search term (like health benefits), while the Description would be used to include some of the niche vocabulary.

Combined, the Title and Meta Description tags would work together to cover the most important words and phrases related to my article.

The Meta Keyword Tag

The Meta Keyword tag is a place where you can list keywords and key phrases related to your web page.

In the source code, it looks like this:

<meta name="keywords" content="Keyword1, keyword 2, etc">

A few years ago, search engines actually used the Meta Keyword tag as a ranking factor, and so took notice of the words and phrases inside it. Today however, the search engines do not give you any boost in rankings for this tag. It is my belief that search engines may use it to spot spammers and award penalties to those who still think it might be a ranking factor.

Any page that has a keyword stuffed Meta Keyword tag is breaking the webmaster's guidelines as laid down by Google. I also believe that webmasters who do this are penalized, depending on the extent and frequency that they try to exploit this tag.

I personally do not use this tag on my sites and do not recommend you bother with it either. If you do want to use it, make sure you only include a small number of keywords. Note too, that they must relate to your content, meaning every single word or phrase you include in this tag is actually on your web page (important).

Let's have a quick look at the Meta Keywords used by the top five sites for the krill oil search term.

1. krill oil, effectiveness, satisfaction, ease of use, uses, user ratings, user reviews, side effects, safety, interactions, medical information, medical advice, natural treatment, warnings, products

2. Does not use the Meta Keyword tag.

3. omega 3, krill oil, sources of omega 3, benefits of krill oil, omega 3 deficiency, omega 3 benefits, dha and epa

4. triglycerides, krill oil, triglyceride levels, krill oil vs fish oil, krill oil benefits

5. Krill Oil side effects

It is interesting to see that the pages ranked #3 and #4 are from the same website. Therefore, Google is ranking two articles from the same site for the search term **health benefits of krill oil**. What I want you to look at are the Titles, Meta Descriptions and Keywords for both of these articles.

See how they are both unique and tailored to the main topic of the article. This is something you need to do on your own site. Every page, even if it is a similar topic to another page, MUST have a unique title, Meta description and Meta keywords (if you use them).

Headlines on Your Page

As a webmaster, you obviously have control over the headlines in your "on-page" content. You have several sizes of headlines, ranging from the biggest H1 header, all the way down to the smallest H6 header.

In your web page source code, an H1 header looks like this:

<H1>Your Headline Here</H1>

In terms of user experience and SEO, I would recommend you only ever use an H1s, H2s and H3s.

H1 is the main headline on your page, and because of this, the search engines give keywords in this heading the most attention. In SEO terms, your H1 headline is the one that has the biggest effect on your page ranking. However, just because it helps to rank your page, don't make the mistake of thinking you can use more than one. Only ever use one H1 header and place it at the very top of your page as the opening title.

Try to get the main keyword for the page into the H1 header, preferably near the start of the headline.

As you write your content, break it up with H2 headers. If an H2 section has sub-sections, use H3s for those titles. I rarely use H3 headers on my own pages as H1 and H2s are sufficient in nearly all cases. Be aware that H2 and H3 have very little effect on rankings, so I don't recommend you try to add keywords to these, unless it makes sense to do so. Just don't go out of your way to add them.

The opening H1 headers for my top five pages ranking for **health benefits of krill oil** are:

1. Find a Vitamin or Supplement.
2. Exciting **Krill Oil Benefits** That Make You **Healthier**, Happier, Younger and Stronger!
3. **Krill Oil**: This Almost Perfect Natural Oil Could Slow Down Your Aging Clock.
4. **Krill Oil** Supplementation Lowers Your Triglycerides.
5. Krill Oil.

The page ranked #1 (WebMD) is again the odd one out here due mainly to its authority, thus making it rank more easily. It does use a second H1 right under the first, and that one is **Krill Oil**. I don't recommend you create two H1 headers on a page. WebMD gets away with it because of Google's tolerance for authority sites.

As you can see from the other four pages, the H1 headers all include **Krill Oil** at or near the beginning of the headline. We've also got other niche vocabulary appearing in these headlines too. Most importantly, make sure your headlines read well for your visitors.

Image Optimization

When you add an image to your page, the source code (in its simplest form) looks like this:

```
<img src="Image URL" alt="ALT Text"/>
```

You might also have width and height parameters as well.

The **Image URL** in that code will be the URL to the image (which includes the image filename). Google can read the image filename in this URL, so it makes sense to help Google out and tell them what the image is. If the image is a bottle of krill oil, call the file "bottle-of-krill-oil.jpg". If it's an image of krill in the sea, call it "krill-swimming-in-sea.jpg", or whatever else helps to best describe the image. The opportunity is clearly there to insert a keyword, but don't overdo it. Only insert the most important word or phrase.

The other important part of this code is the ALT text. This is the text shown in browsers when images are turned off (not visible to the user). It's also the text that is read by text-to-speech software, often used by those with sight impairment. Use the ALT tag to describe the image with these users in mind. You can put a keyword in there, but again, don't stuff them.

A couple of the top five pages in Google ranking for "health benefits of krill oil" have used images. Let's look at the source code of those images. Here I have cleaned up the HTML code so that you can only see the filename and ALT tag):

1. `<img src="/krill-oil-hand.jpg" alt="krill-oil-hand">`

2. `<img src="/krill-oil-beats-common-diseases.jpg" alt="krill oil beats common diseases">`

You will notice that the filename and the ALT tag in each example are the same. This is fine and I actually recommend you do this as well.

You may want to experiment by creating a different filename and ALT tag for an image. However, if you do, I suggest you don't use different keywords in each. Both of these should contain the same description, one for the search engine and the other for visually impaired users. If Google thinks you are trying to get different keywords into the filename and ALT tags of the same image, they might label you a spammer. At the end of the day, it's just easier to use the same sentence for filename and ALT tag, and it looks more natural too.

Spelling & Grammar

If the spelling and grammar is bad on your site, visitors will not be overly impressed. This can lead to higher bounce rates and less time spent on the site. For no other reason that this, it's a good idea to check both.

Google views spelling and grammar as quality signals. The odd mistake won't make a difference, but pages with lots of errors will probably not rank too well in the long-term. A site that has lots of pages with poor grammar and spelling throughout is unlikely to rank for anything much.

Links on the Page

Your web pages will include links to other web pages. These web pages may be on the same site (internal links), or point to pages on a different website (external links).

Over the course of time, web pages may be moved or get deleted. It is important, therefore, to check links periodically to make sure they don't become broken or dead links.

The most common broken links on a page tend to be external links, since we have no control over pages run by other webmasters. They can remove or rename their pages without notice, and when they do, your link becomes broken.

Fortunately, there is a good free tool that can check for broken links on your site called Xenu Link Sleuth.

http://home.snafu.de/tilman/xenulink.html

This tool will find all broken links, both internal and external.

Internal links on your site can also get broken if you rename a page, or delete one. I use a lot of internal linking on my sites to help visitors navigate, and also to help Google spider, or crawl, my content. Changing a filename of a page could break dozens of links, or hundreds even, if you run a large site. To prevent this from happening, I use an internal linking plugin that automates the linking of words and phrases to pages. If I rename or delete a page, I can simply change the settings in the internal linking plugin and all the internal links on my site then update automatically.

You can read more about the internal linking plugin that I use, and how I go about my internal linking here:

http://ezseonews.com/int-link

But what about linking out to other websites? Is that a good or bad idea?

Well, linking out to other websites is natural. Think about writing a research paper for a minute. It's natural to cite other papers as your source of reference, and you do that by linking to those references.

Similarly, when you create an article for your site, it's natural to "cite" other web pages by linking to them. These might be pages you used for research, or pages you found interesting and relevant to your own content. In other words, they are pages that you think your visitors would appreciate you sharing with them.

The one thing you need to be aware of is that links to other site's pages are votes for them. If those other pages are spammy or low quality, those links can actually hurt you. This is because Google assumes you are voting for spam, and may be in some way connected with the pages you link out to. After all, why would you otherwise bother?

Therefore, if you link to a page that you don't necessarily endorse for various reasons, then it is important to use the "nofollow tag" in the link.

The source code of a link with the nofollow tag looks like this.

<a href="Theothersite.com" rel="nofollow">The Other Site</a>

I personally use the "nofollow" tag for the vast majority of all outbound links. Unless of course, the site I'm linking to is a recognized high authority site within my niche. In these cases, I'll usually leave the nofollow out because I want Google to associate my site with these authority sites. In other words, I'm telling Google that I endorse these sites.

While we are on the subject of "nofollow", if you allow visitors to comment on your content (recommended), then make sure their links are all "nofollow". That includes any link used in the comment itself, and any URL that they include in their mini profile, which typically links to the commenter's name and points to their own websites.

Note that the "nofollow" approach will probably mean you get fewer comments than a site that doesn't use the "nofollow" tag. This is because other webmasters see very little in it for them if Google ignores their link. However, if you don't do this, you'll quickly find that as the comments build up, you will get dozens and then hundreds of outbound links – site-wide - to pages you have no control over, and no idea of their quality or reputation. The "dofollow" approach, on the other hand, would probably get you a Google penalty in time, plus a heap of unwanted SPAM comments.

Spying on Competitors for Content Ideas

One of my favourite ways of generating content ideas is to spy on my competitors to see what they are adding to their website.

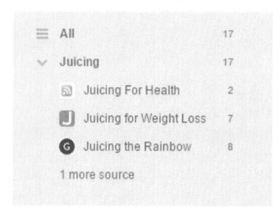

The easiest way of doing this is to subscribe to your competitor's RSS feed, and then monitor that for new content.

If you collect RSS feeds from several competitors, you can enter them all into a single "collection" (one RSS feed) using a service like Feedly. Feedly then notifies you of any new content, across all of the sites, as it's uploaded.

You can see from the above image how I have added three feeds from three different websites, all related to juicing, into a collection I aptly named "Juicing". If I click on the "Juicing" item in the menu, it shows me new content from all of those feeds in the collection:

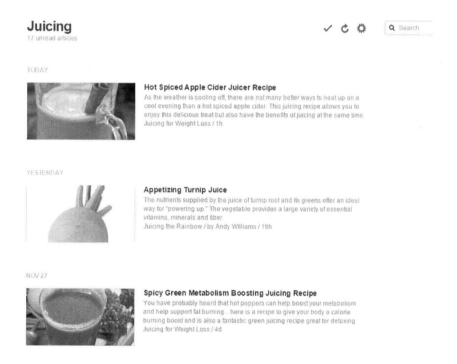

This really is a great way to find new content ideas. Let your competitors do the research to find out what their readers want, then apply their ideas to your own site. Another upside of this is that you can be the first to comment on their new articles, and that can lead to more traffic to your site.

You can extend this method by using Google Alerts to monitor keywords in your niche.

If, for example, you had a website about bee colony collapse, you could set up an alert at Google for that. So whenever new items appear in the SERPs that relate to bee colony collapse, you get notified right away. Notifications can be sent via email, or they can be included in an RSS feeds, which you can then add to your Feedly account. Once set up, you have your finger firmly on the pulse in your niche, and any breaking news in it gets delivered to you right away, ready for your own "breaking news" article that you can post on your site. Share any new story via social media, and you can quickly find these articles attracting both backlinks and traffic.

The topic of web content could actually fill a book of its own. In fact, I have written a book called "Creating Fat Content" which extends the ideas here, and is available on Amazon. See section at the end of this book if you want a link.

2. Site Organization

What Google Tells Us About Site Design

Google gives us a lot of information about site design, which we should consider as best practices. Put another way, Google knows how their search engine works, and therefore knows the site design elements that work best for them.

Google lists all these Standards in its Google Webmaster Guidelines, but let's go through some of the important points here.

1. Create a Sitemap

Google wants you to create a sitemap and submit it to their Webmaster Tools, and I recommend you do this. If you are using WordPress, there are many plugins which can create sitemaps automatically for you.

Google also suggests that you have a sitemap for visitors as it helps guide them to relevant parts of your site. I actually think this is less important than a sitemap for the search engines, since a good navigation system on the site (plus a good search facility) will do that job for you. It is my experience that users would rather use an intuitive navigation system, one that effortlessly guides them around the site's pages, than a long list of hyperlinks in a sitemap.

2. Make Sure Your Site Has a Clear Hierarchy

We'll look at the hierarchical structure of the site soon, but for now, just know that Google expects EVERY page on your site to be reachable through a static link on another page (not necessarily the sitemap). I'd go one step further in suggesting that every page on your site should be no more than two clicks from the homepage, and the more important pages no more than one click away from the homepage.

3. Keep Links on a Page to a Reasonable Number

Search engines can actually spider every link on a page, even very long ones, so I can only assume this guideline is for the benefit of users. If you have certain "calls to action" that you want visitors to make, the fewer links (and other distractions) there are the better.

4. Dynamic Pages Vs Static Pages

Dynamic pages often contain the "?" character before some parameters. Google suggests you try to make static pages rather than dynamic pages, though if you have to use dynamic pages, try to keep the parameters to a bare minimum.

5. A Robots.txt File?

Robot.txt files is used to set rules for your site, e.g. stopping search engine spiders from crawling specific pages; effectively hiding them from the SERPs.

A robots.txt file sits in the root folder of your site and basically contains a series of allow or disallow commands, telling spiders/crawlers which pages they can and cannot access. Google suggests that if you have pages on your site that you do not want spiders to crawl, then use a robots.txt file. If, on the other hand, you want the spiders to crawl every page on your website, then do not create a robot.txt file, not even a blank one.

If you are a WordPress user, you may be wondering about all of the script files and folders. My advice here is to check out yoast.com for the latest advice on WordPress robots.txt files. With the Yoast SEO plugin, you can easily control which pages Google shows in its search results, and which pages it doesn't, all done from within your WordPress Admin area. Here is a link to the article:

https://yoast.com/wordpress-robots-txt-example/

6. Check Your Site in Different Browsers

Unfortunately, different web browsers can display a page very differently. It is therefore wise to check your site in a range of different browsers to make sure it looks good for everyone, irrespective of what browser they are using. You might not be able to get your site looking perfect in every single web browser (there are a lot of them around these days) but you want it to at least look good in the top five, namely Google Chrome, Mozilla Firefox, Microsoft Internet Explorer (soon to be replaced by Microsoft Edge (codenamed Spartan), Opera, and Apple Safari).

Do a Google search for **browser compatibility testing** for various free services that allow you to test your site in a variety of browsers.

At the very minimum, you should check in mobile browsers. A responsive theme is a must-have these days. Responsive themes adjust how your site displays, depending on the browser resolution of the visitor. At the time of writing, between 45%-60% of my own site visitors (for a variety of sites) are coming in on mobile devices.

For WordPress users, I used to recommend a plugin that switched themes for mobile users. However, the themes it produced were a little crude. I now recommend that you buy a responsive theme. I personally use the Genesis theme framework. You can see a range of themes that use Genesis here:

http://ezseonews.com/studiopress

On that page, click the "Shop for Themes" link in the top navigation menu.

Look for the themes labelled **HTML 5** as these are the responsive options. You can click those theme thumbnails to get more details and to see a demo of each one.

Try loading some of those themes in your desktop computer, your tablet and your phone, or use an online browser emulator if you don't have access to multiple devices. See how each theme changes the site design according to the screen dimensions of your device?

This type of responsive theme will keep mobile users happy, without compromising the experience of desktop visitors.

7. Monitor Your Site Load Times

Site visitors will not hang around if your pages take a long time to load. Therefore, don't add unnecessary bloat to your pages. Create light, fast-loading pages with optimized images to make sure they load as quickly as possible. Page load speed is certainly a factor used in the Google algorithm, and although it is not a major one, it is still worth noting.

I personally use a free service for checking page load speeds. Here is the link:

http://gtmetrix.com

We'll come back and look at this tool in more detail later in the book.

OK, so those are the guidelines from Google specifically about site structure. I recommend you head on over to the Google Webmaster Guidelines and familiarize yourself with them all. Seriously, they'll help to keep you on the right side of Google.

A Note About Exact Match Domain Names

An exact match domain (EMD) is one that uses the main keyword phrase you are targeting as the domain name, e.g. buyviagraonline.com (if you wanted to target "buy Viagra online"). Typically, EMD websites target very few keywords, placing all their eggs firmly in the "EMD phrase" basket.

If you are starting a new website, choosing a domain name will be the first task you'll need to do. Many people who teach SEO will still tell you to go for an EMD because it offers ranking advantages over non-EMDs. This was true in the past, but not now. In fact, on September 28, 2012, Google released an update that aimed to reduce the ranking ability of poor quality EMDs.

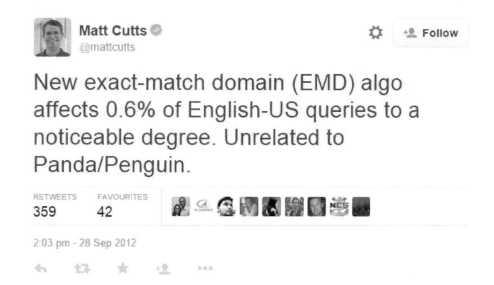

This news shouldn't have come as a surprise to the more switched on SEOs because two years earlier, Google's Matt Cutts announced that the company would be looking at why

EMDs ranked so well when he spoke at Pubcon, Las Vegas, in November, 2010.

The problem with EMDs today is that Google scrutinises them more closely. This means there's always an added risk of them receiving penalties, whether they deserve it or not. Because of this, I recommend you look for a brandable domain name instead, and try to find one that people will remember easily.

What Is a Low Quality EMD, Exactly?

I would say that any EMD that is not a brand or company name is at risk of being labelled low quality. The reason is simply that site owners choose EMDs to rank for a particular phrase.

Webmasters have traditionally looked at their keyword research and found a phrase that is commercially attractive, that is, low competition, high search volume, and high AdWords Cost per click. Once found, they register the phrase as an EMD. Their sole intention is to then rank well for the phrase and monetise the webpage(s) using Google AdSense. Any website that is setup with the primary goal of ranking for a single phrase is a glorified doorway page, and we know what Google thinks of those.

One thing that makes a lot of these low quality EMDs stand out is the high percentage of backlinks that use the exact same keyword phrase as the anchor text. The problem for EMD owners is that using one phrase over and over is largely unavoidable. This is because it's the name of the website, and therefore creates many of the same-looking links pointing back to the page. This is why I suggest you avoid them, unless it is your company/brand name.

Summary: Any EMD that you choose solely for its potential profit is likely to cause you problems going forward.

Good Site Structure

The way you structure your site is extremely important, not only for the search engines, but also for human visitors. Good organization, coupled with a clear and intuitive navigation system, is not only practical, but vital.

From a human point of view, it makes sense that content on a similar topic can be accessed from the same section of the site. For example, if you have a website selling bicycles, then all the mountain bikes should be grouped together, all of the road bikes in another section, and maybe bikes for children in yet another part of the site.

If a young, 22 year old mountain bike rider came to your site, he or she should be able to browse the mountain bike stuff without seeing road racers or children's bicycles distracting their viewing.

If you're using WordPress as a site builder, then organizing your site like this is extremely easy. You simply create a category for each section and assign posts to the most logical category. While it is possible to assign a post to more than one category, I recommend the one-post to one-category approach. This makes for a tighter organization (a better silo), and serves the webmaster, the site visitor, and the search engines, better. If you need to categorise your articles further, e.g. having all 26-inch frame bikes on the same page, then use tags instead of additional categories for the frame sizes. We will look at tags a little later.

This type of "silo" structure works very well for the search engines because it helps them categorize your content. Think of a site that has reviews on the following bikes and accessories.

- Allen Deluxe 4-Bike Hitch Mount Rack
- GMC Denali Pro Road Bike
- GMC Denali Women's Road Bike
- GMC Topkick Dual-Suspension Mountain Bike
- Hollywood Racks E3 Express 3-Bike Trunk Mount Rack
- Kawasaki DX226FS 26-Inch Dual Suspension Mountain Bike
- Mongoose Exile Dual-Suspension Mountain Bike
- Pacific Stratus Men's Mountain Bike
- Topeak Explorer Bike Rack
- Victory Vision Men's Road Bike

If you were to put these into related group (silos), those silos would look something like this.

Silo 1 - Mountain Bikes

GMC Topkick Dual-Suspension Mountain Bike
Kawasaki DX226FS 26-Inch Dual Suspension Mountain Bike
Mongoose Exile Dual-Suspension Mountain Bike
Pacific Stratus Men's Mountain Bike

Silo 2 Road Bikes

GMC Denali Pro Road Bike
GMC Denali Women's Road Bike
Victory Vision Men's Road Bike

Silo 3 Car Racks

Allen Deluxe 4-Bike Hitch Mount Rack

Hollywood Racks E3 Express 3-Bike Trunk Mount Rack

Topeak Explorer Bike Rack

To illustrate how this looks in graph form, the overall structure of the site would now look like this:

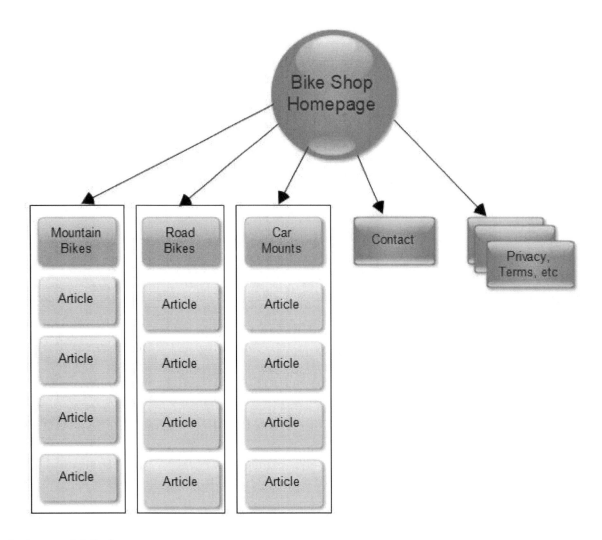

Internal Links

One of the most overlooked pieces of the SEO puzzle is internal linking. This not only helps the search engines to spider your pages more easily, but it also helps visitors find other related content within your site.

With WordPress, there are plugins that can help you automate some of the internal linking on your site. For example "Yet Another Related Posts Plugin", that's YARPP to its friends, is a free WordPress plugin that will automatically create a related posts section at the end of every article on your site.

https://wordpress.org/plugins/yet-another-related-posts-plugin/

You can configure YARPP so that it can only find related posts within the same category. This helps to create a tighter, more natural silo, when articles link to related content on your site.

Here is an example of a "Related Posts" section created by YARP:

Related Posts

> Curcumin, the powerful antioxidant found in Turmeric
Turmeric contains an active ingredient called Curcumin. This active agent has amazing health benefits.

> Turmeric as a powerful antioxidant
Turmeric contains curcumin, a powerful antioxidant. In this video, Dr. Mercola discusses the benefits and properties of curcumin.

This example shows related posts in the sidebar of the site. However, a great place to include them is at the end of the actual article. That way, when your visitor has finished reading one article, they immediately see a list of related articles that might also interest them. This helps to keep visitors on your site for longer.

Linking Pages on a Site Together

Another form of internal linking, which I think is extremely important, is links within the body of your actual articles.

For instance, if you are writing an article about the "GMC Topkick Dual-Suspension Mountain Bike", you might like to compare certain features of the bike to the "Mongoose Exile Dual-Suspension Mountain Bike". When you mention the name of the Mongoose Exile bike, it would help your visitors if you linked that phrase to your Mongoose Exile review. This would also allow the search engines find that article, and help them determine what it's about, based on the link text.

This type of internal linking helps to increase indexing of your site, as well as the rankings of individual pages.

To read more about internal linking, I recommend you read:

Internal Linking & SEO

http://ezseonews.com/backlinks/internal-linking-seo/

Tags - Another Way to Categorise Your Content

Tags are another way to categorize content if you are running a WordPress (or similar content management system) site.

When you write a post, you can include a number of these tags, which further helps to categorize the piece.

For example, if you wrote a post about the "Dyson DC 33 Animal" vacuum cleaner, you would probably put it in the category "Dyson", as that is the most logical "navigation label" for your visitors.

However, you might also want to offer your visitors an easy way to find vacuums that use the Dyson Ball technology, or contain a HEPA filter. So rather than have a separate category for "Dyson Ball" and another for "HEPA filter" (and put the DC33 Animal in all three categories), a better way would be to create tags for this extra classification.

Here are some "tags" you might use on the vacuum site:

- Upright
- Dyson Ball
- Pet hair
- HEPA filter
- Bagless

These tags will help to categorise the posts within the Dyson category, along with every other brand name category on your site.

WordPress actually creates a page for each of these tags, and each of these tag pages can actually rank quite well in Google.

Let's look at an example.

These four vacuums all have a HEPA filters:

1. Eureka Boss Smart-Vac Upright.

2. Hoover Windtunnel

3. BISSELL Cleanview Helix Upright Vacuum Cleaner

4. Miele S2 Series Lightweight

The first vacuum will be in the Eureka CATEGORY with all other Eureka vacuums.

The second vacuum will be in the Hoover CATEGORY with all other Hoover vacuums.

The third vacuum will be in the Bissell CATEGORY and, the fourth vacuum will be in the Miele CATEGORY.

All four vacuums are tagged with "HEPA filter", so will also appear on the HEPA Filter "tag page".

Additionally, the first three vacuums would also appear on the "Upright" tag page.

When people visit your site, they'll be able to narrow down their choice by Brand (using category navigation), or by looking for specific features (using tags to navigate).

A Word of Warning!

I advise you to use tags wisely and sparingly. Don't tag every post with hundreds of tags. Think about your tags carefully and only include the most relevant ones for each post.

The Use and Misuse of Tags

A lot of people do not really understand the significance of tags, and see them as a "keyword list" similar to the Meta Keywords tag. To that end, they create long tag lists for each post. Here is a screenshot of some tags assigned to one post I saw:

Tags: advantages disadvantages of solar power, advantages of a solar panels, advantages of solar cell panel, are MONOCRYSTALLINE sollar pannels good, best mono solar panel price, best quality monocrystaline solar panels, bestpv panels mono or poly, buy pv panels monocrystalline, compare monocrystalin policrystalin photovoltaic, compare monocrystaline and polycrystalline, compare monocrystalline and polycrystalline pannel, compare pollycrystalline vs. monocrystaline modules, crystal cells for solar panels, crystal solar, crystalline si solar efficiency, crystalline solar best, crystalline solar cell technology, crystalline solar cells cost, crystalline solar panels, crystalline solar plate cost, crystalline solar pv module, csun mono-crystalline panels, describe 2 advantages of solar cells, difference between mono and polycrystalline, difference between monocrystalline, difference monocrystalline polycrystalline solar, difference solar panels polycrystalline &, disadvantage to many solar panels, ecokes monocrystalline, ecokes photovoltaic panels, ecokes solar panel, electricity, energy, how i get Monocrystalline silicon, how many rating monocrystalline cell, how Monocrystalline cells are made, how to produce monocrytaline silicon, http://www.monocrystal photo cells/, is monocrystalline better than polycrystalline, is monocrystalline PV best, LUXOR Solar Mono Crystal Dickschichtmodule, maker of monocrystalline panels, mon vs poly efficiency, mono and poly crystalline, mono crystalline pv panels, mono or poly solar panels, mono silicon solar panels, mono solar panel dimensions, mono solar power, mono v poly solar panels, mono versus poly crystalling panels, mono vs poly crystalline panels, mono vs. multicrystalline solar panel, Mono-

This was actually only about 25% of the total tags listed on that page. It just kept scrolling down and down. In SEO terms, this is bad practice. Very bad!

To understand why long tag lists are a bad idea, let's look at what happens when you create a post.

When you publish a post (article) on your blog, WordPress will put that same post onto several pages of your site, including:

1. A page specially created to show the post (the main page).
2. The category page.
3. The author page.
4. For every tag assigned to the post, that post will appear on the corresponding tag page. So if you tag a post with 25 tags, it means that post duplicates across 25 tag pages.

Can you see how that one post now duplicates on multiple pages of your site?

Duplicated Content on a Site Is NOT Good!

Another big problem with using too many tags occurs when only one post uses a particular tag. In that case, the tag page will only have the one article on it, meaning it is almost identical to the main post page created by WordPress for that article.

How to Use WordPress Tags Properly

Get into the tag mindset. Before you use a tag on a post, think about the tag page that will be created for that post.

Your article will appear on each of those tag pages you tag it too. So when you create a new tag for a new post, you have to ask yourself whether you will use this tag on other, relevant posts. The rule of thumb is to never create a tag if it is unlikely to get used by several other posts on your site.

With this in mind, here is what I suggest you do:

During the design stages of your site, make a list on a piece of paper of all the tags you want to use (you can add/edit this list as you build out your site, but at least have a list you can refer to). As you create posts on your site, refer to the tag list you wrote down, and use only tags on that list. By all means add new tags over time, but make sure the tags are going to be used more than once. Don't create a tag that will only ever be used for a single post on your site. Also, only use a few of the most relevant tags for each post.

Finally, never use a word or phrase for a tag that is (or will be) the same as a category name. After all, WordPress will create pages for each category as well; so think of tags as an "additional" categorization tool at your disposal.

Fortunately, there are a number of good plugins to help manage tags if you work with WordPress. Just visit the Plugin directory and search for "Tag Manager". Choose one that has good reviews and works with your current version of WordPress.

Modifying Tag Pages?

Quite often, you will find that your tag pages are getting traffic from Google. I have found that the tag pages often rank very well for the chosen tag (as a keyword phrase).

I like to modify my tag pages (and category pages) by adding an introductory paragraph to each one. The Genesis theme templates have a built in feature that makes this very easy, for category pages as well tag pages.

http://ezseonews.com/genesis

When created this way, the tag pages have an introduction, followed by a list of all related articles (those tagged with that particular tag). This helps to make your tag pages unique, but it also allows you to add more value to your site.

Used properly, tag pages can work for you. Used without thought, tag pages can increase duplicate content on your site and therefore increase your chances of a Google penalty.

3. Authority

What Is An "Authority" Site?

If you go over to the Free Dictionary website and search for authority, there are many different definitions. The highlighted definition below is probably the most apt regarding websites:

au·thor·i·ty 🔊 (ə-thôr'ĭ-tē, ə-thŏr'-, ô-)

n. pl. **au·thor·i·ties**

1.
> a. The power to enforce laws, exact obedience, command, determine, or judge.
> b. One that is invested with this power, especially a government or body of government officials: *land titles issued by the civil authority.*

2. Power assigned to another; authorization: *Deputies were given authority to make arrests.*

3. A public agency or corporation with administrative powers in a specified field: *a city transit authority.*

4.
> a. An accepted source of expert information or advice: *a noted authority on birds; a reference book often cited as an authority.*
> b. A quotation or citation from such a source: *biblical authorities for a moral argument.*

To make your website an authority site, it has to be an **"accepted source of expert information or advice"**.

A well-organized site with excellent content is a great start (the first two pillars of good SEO). However, those two pillars are not enough to make your site an authority. The reason for this is because no one would have heard about you or your fabulous site just yet, and no visitors means zero votes.

Your site (or your own name if YOU personally want to be the authority) MUST be well-known in your particular niche.

So how do you get to be well-known?

Answering that is the easy part. You need to put your site's name and your own face out there, and on as many relevant, high quality places as you can, with links pointing back to relevant pages on your site. In other words, you need "quality" backlinks.

Getting backlinks used to be easy, but with Penguin on the prowl, backlinks is now an area that can quickly get you penalized. This is especially the case if your site is relatively new or doesn't have much authority yet.

There is another aspect of this that I want to discuss before we go into details on back-linking, and that is linking out from your site to authority sites within your niche. We have looked at this earlier in the book, but I want to bring it up again here, just to reinforce the point.

We are all part of a huge web of interlinked websites. If you were talking about something in your niche, it makes sense that you reference other authority websites.

Let's look at an example of this.

If a search engine was trying to evaluate your page on say the Atkins Diet, don't you think that links to other people's studies on the diet, as well as medical references, etc., would help make your page more of an authority? Of course it would, as long as your own content was also excellent. It would also help instil confidence in your visitor by giving them additional value.

So when you write content for your website, don't be afraid to link to other authority sites if they have relevant information that expands on what you've referenced in your own article. Don't use "nofollow" on links to well-known authority sites either, as that just tells the search engine you:

(a) Don't trust the site you are linking to, or

(b) You are trying to hoard the link juice on your own site.

I recommend you get these links to open in a new window, or tab, so that your visitors do not lose your site if they click those links. What you may even decide to do is have a reference section at the end of your post, with active hyperlinks pointing to other authority sites. This way they get to read the entire post without distraction.

In short, do link out to other authority sites, but only when it makes sense and you think it will help your visitor.

OK, that's outbound links sorted.

Links Coming into Your Site

Backlinks to a website are a very important part of the Google algorithm. It's the main reason webmasters build links to their own websites; to help them rank better. However, there is something very important that you need to know about link building. It's not something that most SEO books or courses will tell you about, mainly because they want to sell you their link building tools, or get you to buy recommended tools through their affiliate links. Here's what they don't want you to know:

Google don't want you building links to your site.

In actual fact, we can probably state this a little more strongly than that.

Google HATES you building links to your site.

Google are on the warpath against "webspam" and "link schemes". This includes "unnatural" links. Any link that was created purely to help your page rank higher in the SERPs, and/or links YOU have total control over, is considered as an **unnatural link**.

Properties of an unnatural link include any link where you, as the webmaster:

1. Choose the link text.
2. Choose the destination page.
3. Choose which page the link appears on.
4. Choose where on the page the link appears.

So is every link you have built to your site unnatural? No, it's not. Any link that you create, and would have created even if the search engines did not exist, is not unnatural.

An example of this is if you write an article for an authority site and put a link to your site in the author's bio. This is considered a natural link, since you are the expert who wrote the article and people may want to know where they can find out more about you. You would put that link in there even if there were no search engines.

The term "unnatural" is used by Google to describe those links you created to boost the position of your page in the SERPs. It's a fine dividing line. However, the penalties for crossing that line can be severe.

If Google find links that you have created for your site with the sole purpose of helping it to rank better, they will ignore those links at best, but they will more than likely penalise your site, especially if there are lots of them, site-wide.

You need to bear this in mind as you build links to your web pages.

It can be tempting to go over to the dark side of SEO. There are many people out there who will show you proof that keyword-rich anchor text links still work (usually just before selling you a link-building tool or service). What they don't show you is what happens to that page in the medium to long-term. This type of link building can still give good results in the short-term, but only until Google catches you. It's necessary for you to understand that in 2015 and beyond, it is Google's automated software that hunts you down, and it does a very efficient job at it too.

In this book, I'll only cover what I consider the best long-term strategies for link building; those that look natural to Google.

Here is the general concept of link building:

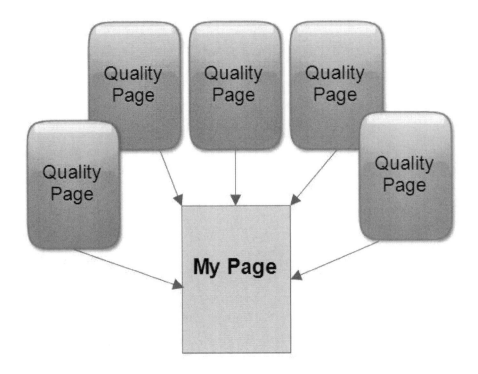

Search Rankings Increase

As you build quality links to your page it will move up the search engine rankings.

Some people will tell you that it doesn't matter whether inbound links are on related pages (to your page) or not. That may have been the case several years ago, but it's certainly not the case now.

If you had a website on "breeding goldfish" and you had 100 inbound links to your site, yet 95% of them were on pages that talked about things like:

- Prescription drugs
- Viagra
- Auto maintenance
- Wedding speeches
- Golf Equipment
- Other, unrelated pages

What is that telling the search engines?

I think Google would look at these backlinks and conclude you were involved in back-linking schemes to help your pages rank better. As we saw earlier, Google's webmaster guidelines tell us that this is a quick road to a penalty.

If the search engines want to use inbound links as a measure of authority, then obviously the most authoritative links you could get would be from quality pages that were on the same or similar topic to the page they linked to.

With Google Penguin, this may be even more important as Google appears to be giving less weight to the anchor text and more weight to the actual THEME of the webpage (or site) that the link is on. Therefore, look for links from pages and sites that are relevant to your own niche, and look for quality sites to get your links.

Always consider quality as a priority in every backlink you get. So the backlink should be on a quality page, and on a quality site. The page on your site should also be quality.

What I have described here is perhaps a little scary. If bad backlinks can get your site penalized, then what is to stop your competitors building poor quality backlinks to you site? Well, this does actually happen, and Google call it **negative SEO**.

Is Negative SEO Real?

Negative SEO is a term that refers to webmasters/SEOs who build poor quality links to a competitor's website in an effort to get it penalized. Many SEOs agree that since Penguin, negative SEO tactics have become a reality. I actually think it was a reality even before Panda, and one of my own tests certainly provided some evidence for this.

At the start of 2011 (before Panda), I began some aggressive back-linking to a site of mine that was several years old. I wanted to use this as a test, so I set up about 150 blogs (using automation software) that I could use to get backlinks from. Since I controlled these blogs, I controlled the backlinks from them as well, and so had the power to delete them if I needed to.

Once everything was in place, I began to submit content to these 150 sites, with backlinks going to the pages on my test site.

The rankings climbed for several weeks, and so did my traffic as a direct consequence. I was monitoring my page rankings for 85 keywords, and around 60 had reached the top 10 in Google, with a large proportion in the top three.

Then, I woke up one morning to find that Google had penalised my site. In fact, all 85 keywords dropped out of the top 100, rendering them totally useless.

These keywords had been out of the top 100 for eight weeks before I began phase two of my experiment. I deleted all 150 blogs, thereby eliminating all of those spammy backlinks in one hit.

Over the next month, things began to improve slowly. Pages started climbing back into the top 100 to the point where I ended up with 64 of the 85 phrases back in the top 100. Around 42 pages were back in the top 30, and 12 were back in the top 10.

NOTE: My rankings obviously did not return to pre-penalty levels. They were only at those pre-penalty levels because of the backlinks I had built. However, I think it was quite clear that Google had lifted my site penalty once I removed the spammy links.

I also know that an algorithm had applied the penalty and not a human reviewer. Whenever a human reviewer penalises a site, you have to submit a re-inclusion request after you've cleaned up the problems. I didn't have to do that. Once I had removed the backlinks, the rankings returned. This proved to me that the entire process was automated.

If your site gets a penalty today, the chances are it is an algorithmic penalty like in my example. Therefore, fixing the issues will remove the penalty, which is actually great news.

Here is a diagram showing poor backlinks to a page:

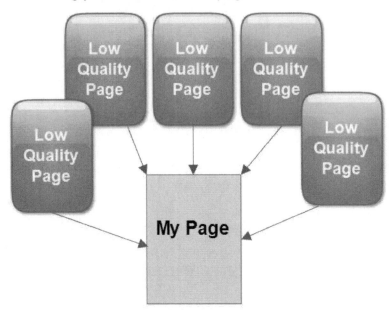

Search Rankings
DECREASE

In this model, poor backlinks actually cause YOUR page to get a Google penalty. The result will be a likely and sudden drop down the rankings.

The point to take home from this is to concentrate on backlinks from good quality, authority sites.

The Type of Backlinks You Should Get

First and foremost, go for QUALITY backlinks every time, not quantity.

For your site to become a real authority, it needs incoming links from other authority websites, blogs and forums. Since Google Penguin, I no longer recommend using any type of automated link building tool.

WHAT?????

I know; I know...

"If I cannot use automated link building tools, how can I get enough links to rank well?"

To answer that question, let me ask you one thing: Do you believe your page DESERVES to rank well based on the **quality of the content** and the **authority of you/your site**?

If you answer "no", then you will have to go down the black hat SEO path to get your page ranked, and ultimately that path will lead to Google penalties, lost rankings, and you having to start over again.

For a page to rank well on your site, you need to make sure it **deserves** to rank well (in terms of content and your site/author authority). After all, you're going to be putting in a lot and time and effort into your new project, and my guess is that you want it to be around for a good while. So make it the best that it can possibly be, and take pride in your site. If you love what you do and share your passion with your visitors, that will start to show naturally on your pages.

Think of it like this example.

You write a page on the "health benefits of vitamin D".

Do you think your page deserves to rank above medical sites, where the authors are medical doctors and trained nutritionists? Google clearly wants to show the most useful and accurate information it can to its customers (web searchers), and that probably means choosing a medical authority site over yours, even if your content happens to be better. You cannot compete on the authority level unless you are an authority on the "health benefits of vitamin D" yourself. That is the way it should be because we all want to find the best, and most relevant information when we search online, and that includes everyone.

How might you gain authority in this area? Well, you could quite simply write articles on vitamin D and have them posted on numerous authority sites, with a link back to your site/page in the author's resource box. Don't try to stick keywords into your backlinks. Use only the title of your site, or the title of the article you are linking to, or the bare URL of the page you are linking to.

When you think about it in these terms, can you understand why I say abandon automated link builders? The links coming into your pages need to be of the utmost quality and professionalism. They need to build your authority, not ruin it by having some tacky computer-generated article with your name on it linking back to your site's pages.

So, with the idea of quality firmly planted in your mind, let me suggest a few places where you can get content published that might actually build your reputation and authority. Before I do that though, I would like to give two general guidelines for back-linking.

1. Only look to get links on authority sites that relate to your own niche.
2. Try to be EVERYWHERE. Whenever someone is searching for information in your niche, make sure they constantly see your name or site cropping up.

It doesn't matter if your link is on a Page Rank zero page, or even PR Unranked. What matters most is that the page resides on a site that has good authority. Two of the only indicators we have for authority are domain age and domain Page Rank, so I suggest you use these while you can (PageRank may well be disappearing soon). Look for domains five years old and older, with domain PR4 or above on the home page. This approach should keep you safe.

Anchor Text?

With Google Penguin, things have changed a lot.

You used to optimize a webpage by including the main keyword phrase in the page title, URL, H1 header and several times in the content. We'd then point lots of backlinks to the page using the main keyword phrase as the anchor text.

Google used to reward this type of optimization.

Then came the Penguin update, and as we've seen, that type of optimization is more likely to get your page/site penalized.

As well as de-optimizing on-page factors, we have also had to de-optimize backlinks to our pages as well. In fact, if you check out the Google Webmaster Guidelines, you'll see this as an example of a "link scheme":

> Links with optimized anchor text in articles or press releases distributed on other sites. For example:
>
> *There are many wedding rings on the market. If you want to have a wedding, you will have to pick the best ring. You will also need to buy flowers and a wedding dress.*

Google are clearly cracking down on keyword-rich anchor text links that point to a webpage. This type of back-linking used to be the norm, and no one thought anything of it. However, when we look at those links now, they really do look spammy, don't they?

Today, we need to be smarter about our backlinks. If we want to survive Google Penguin (and all future algorithm updates), then we cannot create backlinks like we used to. These are the typical types of backlinks created by automated software tools, so that's another compelling reason not to use software to generate backlinks for your site.

NOTE: I don't believe that Google will penalise a web page that has a few backlinks like this. For example, if your web page was about dog training, and 1% of your incoming backlinks used the anchor text "dog training collars", I think that would be fine. However, if 50% or more of your backlinks used "dog training collars" as the anchor text, then that would be an issue and likely raise a red flag.

The Google tolerance for this type of link has been shifting. Google seem to be losing all patience for keyword rich anchor text, especially in the body of articles on other websites. I would even suggest that it is now dangerous to have even 10% of the links to a specific page use the same keyword phrase. Tomorrow, next week or next year, that might drop to 5%, who knows. The point is this: the cleaner we are today, the less we will have to fear tomorrow.

Over time, Google is becoming much less tolerant, and with their disavow tool, they can do this with a clear conscience. At the start of 2013, a study was released showing this tolerance shift. The study showed that:

1. When the Penguin was first released, Google did not penalize sites even when 90% of incoming links were spammy.
2. By June 2012, Google would only tolerate 65% spammy links before issuing a penalty.
3. By October 2012, Google's would only tolerate 50% spammy links before issuing a penalty.

That 50% figure was just TWO YEARS ago, at the time of writing. How much further has Google's tolerance shifted? How low will this percentage go? That's anybody's guess, of course, but I have personally stopped all keyword-focused anchor text links to my own sites.

Do you have a site where you've done this in the past? If so, then you need to be careful and water down the percentage of anchor text rich links if that site is still live. Add in new links on authority sites, using article titles and URLs as the link text. Remove any poor links that you can, and disavow those that you cannot control.

You may be wondering what the current safe level is for keyword-rich anchor texts. To be honest, I don't believe there is a safe level anymore. If there is, it appears to be a moving target; moving in the wrong direction.

Let me go over what I think would be fairly safe limits.

I would recommend a link profile to a page on your site where:

1. NO MORE than 5% of backlinks use commercial keyword-rich anchor text. For all new links you build to your site, I'd recommend you no longer use keyword phrases in anchor text. Use the page title (article H1 heading or site title are also OK) of the page you are linking to, or the naked URL of that page. Rely on strong on-page factors to tell Google what the page is about, along with internal linking, using keyword-rich anchor text because this type of link IS natural on site (see earlier discussion about Wikipedia).

2. The remaining 95% of anchor text should be made up of things like the page URL, the page title, the opening H1 header text, and words that are irrelevant to the topic of the article, like "click here", "read this", "read more", "this site", "this blog", "here", etc. The most "natural" anchor texts to use for any link to a page on your site are the page title and URL. Those are the ones I recommend you use the most

What About Existing Keyword Rich Backlinks?

My suggestion, if you have lots of keyword-rich anchor text links to your site, is as follows:

1. Try to change the anchor text from keywords to page titles/URLs or site name.
2. For backlinks on poor quality websites, remove the links altogether. If you cannot get the links removed, consider disavowing them if they are on really poor quality sites.
3. Build more quality backlinks from authority websites that relate to your niche.

Use page titles, headline text, site name or bare URLs as the anchor text. By building better links to your site, it is possible that you can over-power the poorer links. This is not something I would have said six months ago, but something seems to have changed now.

In October 2014, MicrositeMasters.com published a report in the aftermath of Penguin 3.0. The findings of their report were interesting, actually giving webmasters a little more hope.

Key Points Include:

1. Penguin 3.0 seems to be targeting sites that do not have enough good links.
2. Penguin 3.0 does not seem to be punishing sites for bad links, but is instead "erasing" the value of bad links.

Are Google making a U-turn on their policy of penalising pages with bad backlinks? If so, this would be a major change compared to earlier Penguin updates. We know for sure that the early updates actively penalised sites for low quality backlinks.

One clue may come from something Matt Cutts said in the summer of 2014 (For anyone who doesn't know, Matt Cutts is the American software engineer who leads the web spam team at Google). When asked about negative SEO, Matt confirmed that Google was aware of it, and that the **Payday Loan 2.0** update would close some of the loopholes people were using for negative SEO. Does this mean that instead of penalizing websites for bad backlinks, Google are just ignoring those links, making them ineffective for ranking? That would certainly backup the report on MicrositeMasters.

You can read their full report here:

http://www.micrositemasters.com/blog/penguin-3-0-analysis-what-got-hurt-what-didnt-and-3-things-you-need-to-know-to-remain-relevant/

I still don't recommend keyword rich anchor text backlinks from other websites, but this report may suggest we can stop worrying so much about existing poor quality links. Just overpower bad links with good links from now on.

Of course, if you have thousands or even hundreds of thousands of poor backlinks to your site, the disavow tool may be the best approach. In some cases, moving your site to a new domain may be the only option, but you'll then need to start building your site authority from scratch, so this really is a last resort.

Ranking for a Main Keyword Phrase

The old way we did SEO was to find popular search phrases and build pages around those phrases, thus optimizing the page and backlinks for the perfect ranking boost. With SEO of old, we could choose what phrases we wanted to rank for, and then go after those phrases.

This strategy no longer works. As we've already seen, Penguin penalises if it thinks you've over-optimized the on-page or off-page factors for a particular page. With the recent algorithm updates, it is now very hard to optimise a page safely for a specific term.

You can see this if you do a Google search. Many of the pages that rank for any given term do not contain that term in the title. Some don't even include it on the page.

For example, if I search Google for the term '**honey bees dying**', only four pages in the top 100 of Google include that exact phrase in the title. Most don't even include that phrase on the web page itself. The reason these pages rank highly is not because of the keyword phrases on the page, it's because those pages are themed around the topic of "honey bees dying", so they include the words and phrases that Google know should be included in the content. We covered all of this in the section on writing content around a theme, but it's good to mention it again to emphasize its importance.

If you want to rank for a specific phrase, this is the method I use, and the one I suggest you follow:

1. Find theme words used on pages that rank in the top 10 at Google.
2. Write an "epic" post on the topic and theme it with the relevant niche vocabulary. Making sure the page is unique and adds more value than the other pages in the top 10. In other words, I make sure it deserves to be in the top 10.
3. Get backlinks from other authority sites in the niche, using the page title as the link text.
4. Use internal linking to the new page with a variety of link text, including the one I am targeting.

That's it, my four-step process for ranking a page for a specific keyword phrase. The benefit of this strategy is that you can also rank for hundreds of other long-tail keyword phrases.

Back-linking from Now On

Google seem to be paying less attention to inbound anchor text and more attention to the topic of the page that is linking to yours.

For example, if your page is on "Health benefits of curcumin" and you got a link from a page about curcumin or turmeric, then that link would be a valuable one, irrespective of the anchor text used to link to your page.

With that in mind, I'd suggest trying to make your links look as authoritative as possible. Think how academic literature links to another article. They'll use the title of the other article or the bare URL. They might also use the journal name and edition to help find the document. If you were writing a guest post for another website, and with the intention of linking back to your own site, instead of doing this:

> Curcumin has shown remarkable <u>anti-cancer properties</u> not only in stripping the cancer cells defenses to make them more visible to the body's natural immune system, but also in cell apoptosis.

...where **anti-cancer properties** is one of the phrases you want to rank for, and links to your site, do something like this instead:

> Curcumin has shown remarkable anti-cancer properties not only in stripping the cancer cells defenses to make them more visible to the body's natural immune system, but in an article <u>"Curcumin initiates cancer cells death"</u>, the author describes experimental results showing cell apoptosis occurring.

Do you see how natural this looks to a visitor? This looks like a recommendation to read more information on the topic. It looks like something to help the visitor rather than just something used to score points from a search engine. This type of link looks more authoritative, more natural to Google, AND it will be extremely valuable to your site.

If you submit articles to other sites for the purpose of back-linking, then I recommend the following:

4. Use in-context links like the one above, where the link uses the article title (or URL). This way, the reader is in no doubt what the destination page is all about.

5. Place a link to a URL or homepage in the author's resource box. Once again, don't use keyword phrases as the anchor text. Use the URL, the domain name, or the title of the page you are linking to.

With Penguin, we actually need fewer backlinks to rank well, but they need to be from relevant, quality web pages. Google is giving MORE weight to quality links than it used to. Remember, quality over quantity is the key here.

OK, so where can you look for backlinks?

The Best Backlinks

The very best backlinks you can get to your site are the ones you do not create yourself. These are backlinks from other sites that you did not personally request. In other words, another webmaster links to your site because they think it is worthy and offers value to their own visitors. Obviously you don't have any say in the anchor text that is used in these links. They are also the most difficult to get, but they are the best. This is because they are natural votes and you don't have to do anything to get them.

People are constantly linking back to authority websites, which means the owners of those sites don't have to run their own link campaigns.

The **ideal backlinks** to your site would have the following properties:

1. The link is on a high authority site.
2. The page containing the link relates to the page it links to.
3. The page containing the link is a high quality page, with high quality content.
4. The link is in the body of the article (contextual).
5. The link uses your page title for the anchor text.
6. There are very few outbound links (to other websites) on the same page.
7. The page your link appears on has a lot of human interaction (social shares, comments, etc).
8. YOU do not control the backlink.

The Best Way to Get Quality Inbound Links

The best chance you have of getting those Holy Grail backlinks is to develop Epic Content that acts as **"Link Bait"**.

Develop content that your visitors love and want to share with others via their social media channels. Develop content on your site that other site owners will want to link to.

When other people WANT to link to your content, we call that content "link bait", since it attracts links naturally.

The best way of using Link Bait is to develop some awesome content, then make sure you get it seen by posting on social channels, or forums and various other websites. You can do this where people are asking for the answers to questions that your content covers.

So what types of content makes good link bait? I'll tell you my thoughts in a moment, but first, I recommend you read this article by Neil Patel, and then return here:

http://www.quicksprout.com/2015/08/03/the-5-types-of-content-that-attract-the-most-backlinks/

Here is the list that I look to when trying to develop good "link bait".

1. **Infographics** are graphical representations of complex topics. They are favourites for sharing on social channels, e.g. Pinterest. They often get re-posted on other sites, which is great. When you create and post an infographic on your site, you can include the HTML code for other webmasters to copy and paste onto their own sites. This will display the infographic on their site, with a small link back to your own page:

Copy/paste the code below to share this image on your site or blog!

```
<div align="center"><a href="http://www.getnp.com"><img
src="http://www.transparentcorp.com/research/images/beta-brain-wave-infographic.jpg"
width="800" height="3837" /></a><br>Source: <a
href="http://www.transparentcorp.com/research/beta-brain-waves.php">Beta Brain Waves - An
Infographic</a></div>
```

2. **Scripts & tools** that people will bookmark and share with others. Webmasters will always link to useful tools, especially if they are free. Here is one example of a tool that searches for the nutritional information of food:

3.   Another good example is a currency converter script, where you can convert one currency to another. A time zone convertor could prove popular too. There's also a cholesterol conversion tool, converting between the two popular units for cholesterol - mg/dl and mmol/L. Any tool you can create, or have created for you, and that people find useful, will inevitably attract links from other websites, as well as through social sharing.

4.   **Free downloads like software or PDFs** that people find useful. If you can give these away, and people really do find them useful, then they will share your URL with their friends on any forums they frequent, and through their social media channels.

5.   **Posts that include "lists".** People love to share lists on forums, in comments on other blogs, and via their social channels. For example, "Top 10 WordPress Plugins" on a site about building websites would be very interesting to people keen on constructing their own WordPress site. A post like this could get a lot of social shares, plus other sites will link to it. A tip here is to contact the authors of the plugins that you recommend, and tell them that you have made a top 10 list on the advantages of their plugins. Many will link to your post from their own site, to prove to their visitors how useful their plugin actually is.

6. **Controversial posts** are always popular. When people are controversial, they

usually evoke a strong response. I cannot tell you how to be controversial in your own niche, but I would just say, make your controversy factual. Making something up just to be controversial won't work, and it will annoy your visitors too.

A while ago, there was lots of information coming out about how good intermittent fasting was for losing weight, and improving health in general. Everyone was jumping on the bandwagon. One website went against the grain with a headline something like "Intermittent Fasting Is Bad for Women". It caused quite a stir. The important point about this controversy is that it was factual. The article went on to explain that certain types of women developed problems during intermittent fasting (typically those with low body fat). This controversy resulted in a lot of natural backlinks as people debated it on blogs and forums. Of course, it also brought in a lot of extra traffic for the webmaster.

7. **Include a forum.** Let's say, for example, you had a website on "Husky dogs". A forum would attract Husky dog owners, who would then recommend your site to their friends and through their social channels. Building user participation through a forum on your site is a great way to attract natural links. Any member of your forum becomes a potential link builder for you when they are on other sites or talking to friends. Forums are very easy to add to a site using a script (check out vBulletin.com). The downside to forums is that they do take a lot of work to maintain, especially if they become popular.

8. **Interviews.** Interview an expert in your niche, and use that interview to attract inbound links to your site. You needn't buy expensive equipment or software for an interview. A cheap headset and Skype is all you need.

If it is an audio-only interview, post the audio on your site with a transcript of the interview below it. The transcript will act as search engine bait, but apart from that, a lot of visitors actually prefer to read this type of thing rather than listen to it. You can also upload audio interviews to audio sharing sites. Search Google for **audio upload** and look for opportunities where you can create a backlink to your site. You can create a very natural backlink on this type of audio sharing site by saying something like "Prefer a transcript? Read the full interview on..." and then link directly to your transcript page using the title of that page as the anchor text.

If the interview is a video, upload the video to YouTube, and maybe Vimeo and Dailymotion as well. Create a post on your own site and embed the YouTube video. Include the transcript of the video (for the same reasons as above) on your site. In the YouTube description of the video, add the URL where people can "read the transcript". Finally, remember to give the interviewee the page URL so that they can find the video on your site. They will more than likely link to it and possibly tell their own visitors/mailing list about the interview too. It's a great way of attracting a powerful backlink from an authority site in your niche. Attracted links are links you have no control over, and remember, these are the most powerful and natural links a website can get. They will prove your site's worth to the search engines.

I'd choose one link attained in this manner over 1,000 links from traditional back-linking methods.

Broken Link Building

Before we move on to look at the more traditional methods of building links, there is one method that you need to know about which works really well. This approach is 'broken link building'. This essentially means you look for broken links (related to your own site) on other websites. You then contact the owner to tell them about it, offering your own link as a replacement.

As an example, let's consider a website on health and nutrition. If I owned that site, I'd go out looking for websites that have broken links to any articles on health or nutrition. Let's say I find a page about the importance of vitamin A for good eye health, and one of the links on that page goes to a 404 Error - Page Not Found. I would contact the webmaster of the nutrition site, informing them that the link went to a 404 error, and tell them I have a page on the same topic if they need a good replacement source to link out to. Obviously I would include my URL for consideration.

The advantage of this type of link is that it is often on an aged page, possibly on an authority site. A backlink from this type of site would be a good one, added by the other webmaster and giving you no control over the link text, unless of course, the webmaster asked you what would like for the link text.

Let's now take a look at how you would go about finding broken links on related pages.

There are actually a number of tricks we can use for finding broken links.

The first is to search Google for resource/links pages in our niche, using a "footprint". Here are a few that work well:

"KEYWORD links"
"KEYWORD resources"
"KEYWORD web links"
inurl:links "KEYWORD"
Swap out KEYWORD for a phrase that relates to your niche / webpage.

That last one is an interesting search phrase as it looks for webpages that include the word "links" in the URL, and are about your keyword. Here is an example search for that "footprint".

inurl:links "juicing for health"

Web   Images   Videos   News   Shopping   More ▾   Search tools

85 results (0.64 seconds)

● Healthy Links | Juicer Recipes Now
juicerrecipesnow.com/healthy-**links**/ ▾
Juicing for Health- This is one of my favorite juicing websites created by Sara, from
Kuala Lumpur, Malaysia. Contains a lot of information about fruits and ...

● LINKS - JUicing for health
cat125juicing.weebly.com/**links**.html
JUicing for health · JUICING · Purchasing A Juicer · PRODUCE NUTRITION · RED ·
ORANGE/YELLOW · GREEN · BLUE/PURPLE · WHITE · Recipies · FAQ ...

See how the top two results are clearly links pages about "juicing for health"?

Using footprints like this offers the quickest way of finding broken link opportunities.
You first find the links pages and then check them out to see if any links are broken.

Now, before you think you need to go through every link manually, clicking on each of
them to check for a broken link, don't worry, it's not that manual. Let me tell you
about a free Google Chrome extension called **Check My Links.** Search the Google
Chrome store for the plugin and install it.

Once installed, you'll have a button in the toolbar for the extension. Now all you
have to do is visit the page you want to check for broken links, and then click the
extension button. You'll get a badge in the top right of the screen, giving you a
breakdown of the links on the page:

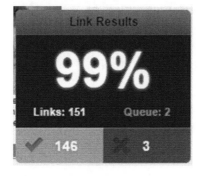

I can see from this badge that three links are broken. Scrolling down the page, the
links are colour coded for easy identification:

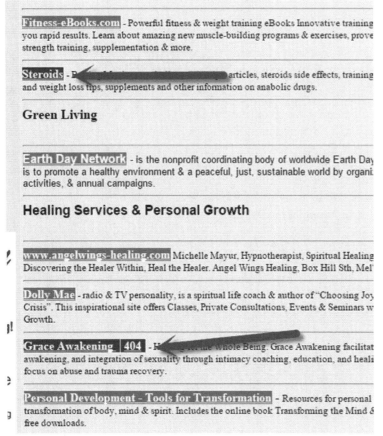

Fitness-eBooks.com - Powerful fitness & weight training eBooks Innovative training you rapid results. Learn about amazing new muscle-building programs & exercises, prove strength training, supplementation & more.

Steroids - ~~Powerful~~ articles, steroids side effects, training and weight loss tips, supplements and other information on anabolic drugs.

Green Living

Earth Day Network - is the nonprofit coordinating body of worldwide Earth Day is to promote a healthy environment & a peaceful, just, sustainable world by organi activities, & annual campaigns.

Healing Services & Personal Growth

www.angelwings-healing.com Michelle Mayur, Hypnotherapist, Spiritual Healing Discovering the Healer Within, Heal the Healer. Angel Wings Healing, Box Hill Sth, Mel'

Dolly Mae - radio & TV personality, is a spiritual life coach & author of "Choosing Joy Crisis". This inspirational site offers Classes, Private Consultations, Events & Seminars w Growth.

Grace Awakening | 404 - H~~~~ Whole Being. Grace Awakening facilitat awakening, and integration of sexuality through intimacy coaching, education, and heali focus on abuse and trauma recovery.

Personal Development - Tools for Transformation - Resources for personal transformation of body, mind & spirit. Includes the online book Transforming the Mind & free downloads.

You can see how easy it is to spot the broken links. If I had a good page on steroids, I'd be writing to this webmaster about swapping out that first link with my own.

But what if my health site did not have a page on steroids?

The answer is simple. I'd create one, providing it was viable of course.

I'd probably head off to the Way Back Machine: http://archive.org/web/ to check out the page that currently has the broken link. This free service shows you what that page looked like in the past.

Although that steroid page no longer exists today, the Way Back Machine keeps cached copies of most pages of most websites. Here is the steroid page as it was back in April 13, 2012:

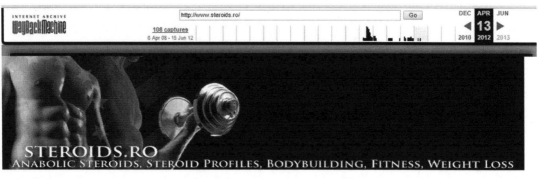

This archived page will give me some ideas for my own steroid page before I contact the webmaster about the broken link.

At the end of the day, if that webmasters ignores me, or just deletes the broken link without using mine, I still have a great new piece of content for my own site.

The easiest broken backlinks to find are on this type of resource page. The reason for this is because these are the types of pages webmasters typically post links to, and for good reason.

I know a lot of SEOs will tell you that links on link resource pages are a waste of time, but that simply is not true. Start judging ALL backlink opportunities by the quality of the page your link will appear on, rather than the type of page. To find out if the page is of value to you, ask the following five questions:

1. Is the page good quality?
2. Does the page only link to sites within a very narrow niche topic?
3. Does the page only link to quality sites?
4. Is the page genuinely useful to visitors of that site?
5. Is the page part of a quality website?

If these guidelines apply, then the page is a good one for your backlink(s).

Broken backlink building is a good way to get quality backlinks on aged, authority pages in your niche; that's if you can find them of course.

The methods mentioned above are my favourite ones for back-linking. However, this chapter would not be complete without looking at the fall-back options.

Traditional Back-linking Sources

Quality backlinks can be difficult to get, so it's a good idea to have a broad plan. I like to create a single piece of content that I can repurpose and develop into other formats. For example, I can create an article on a relevant topic, and from that one article create the following:

1. A text based article for submission to another site.
2. A PDF version for submission to PDF sharing sites.
3. A slideshow presentation of the main points of the article to upload to sites like Slideshare.net.
4. An infographic of the main points.
5. A video using the contents of the article. This can be the slideshow presentation with a voice-over. Alternatively, you could use flexible software like Explaindio to create an animated video or "whiteboard video" of the main points. You can read my brief video review here:

http://ezseonews.com/review/explaindio-2/

From doing one piece of research you now have several different media types to use for backlinks. Let's look at the types of places you can submit these documents to.

NOTE: What follows are the typical backlink resources recommended by most SEO courses and books. Use these with caution. And by the way, I really do suggest you ignore the popular advice to use keyword rich anchor text in your backlinks. Stick with page titles, site name or bare URLs, and try to insert the link so that it looks natural.

Article Directories

This is a strange one because some experts believe that article marketing no longer works. I personally believe that it does still work, although it's nowhere near as effective as it used to be. Worth mentioning also, is to NEVER submit the same article to lots of different directories. A far more productive approach is to pick maybe 10 quality directories (niche specific directories are the best) and submit a unique article to each one.

I know a lot of people are tempted to write an article and use a spinner to generate 100s of unique versions of it to use specifically for article marketing. My advice is don't be tempted. Unique is not just about the words on the page, but the information in the article. A spun article is not only spam, but it also duplicates content in the eyes of Google.

OK, I know what you are thinking. This means you have to write 10 unique articles. Yes, it does, but if you want to be completely "white hat" about this, and build your authority in a way Google cannot object to, then that is what you need to do. This really is the only safe way of doing article marketing. Don't forget too, that once your articles are up, they stay up, and so do your links.

When adding a backlink to your site, do not simply hyperlink a relevant keyword phrase in the article. Remember, Google's webmaster guidelines advise you against this.

- Links with optimized anchor text in articles or press releases distributed on other sites.
  For example:
  There are many wedding rings on the market. If you want to have a wedding, you will have to pick the best ring. You will also need to buy flowers and a wedding dress.

Place any backlinks you create when doing article marketing in the author bio box at the end of your article. I'd recommend you only link to your homepage from these bio boxes, and only by using your site name or site URL as the anchor text. Don't link to an internal page from this type of backlink, and don't link using the homepage title. Stick only to the site name or URL.

If you really want to get a backlink into the body of your article, go back and look at the example I gave you in the "Back-linking from now on" section. Here you will see how to naturally use links in the body of the piece. However, if you do this, do not link to the same site in the author bio box as well. Note also that some article directories will not allow links in the article body, so be sure to check out the site's guidelines first.

For the amount of effort it takes, I'd actually suggest you don't use article marketing as a main strategy. Write the content, and look for guest posting opportunities on relevant sites instead. We'll look at guest posting later in the book.

Forum Participation

Forums have been heavily spammed by webmasters in the past, looking for easy link opportunities. There are two obvious ways to get links from a forum. The first way is by using your forum profile, which usually has a field to enter your website URL. This backlink is a forum profile link. Software exists that can create thousands of forum profile links automatically.

It seems obvious to me that Google can spot this type of linking very easily indeed. Imagine a website gaining 5,000 forum profile backlinks in a matter of days.

Think too about the page this link will sit on. Does it meet any of the requirements for a quality page? In most cases the answer is no. It might be OK if you create a wonderful profile page with lots of content, but to create forum profiles simply for backlinks is a very bad idea. An even worse idea is to use automated software. Abusing forum profile links is a quick way to get penalised by Google.

When it comes to forums, the best way to get good backlinks is to get involved in the forum discussions and help people. Before entering a new niche, I recommend you scout out 2-3 forums that allow backlinks in their forum signatures, and then sign up to join. As you build your site, pop into these forums and start contributing every now and again. By the time your site is ready to go live, you can insert your web URL into your forum signature and get instant backlinks, as well as traffic from the forum visitors who visit your profile; the latter of which will only happen if you become a forum participant.

When you register with the forum, make sure you use your website email address with an attached Gravatar image (check out https://en.gravatar.com/). This image should be a photograph of you; the same one you use on your site. Your image will then appear next to your posts in the forum. People will see your posts on different forums and start to recognize you as that "expert" they've seen before. They will start to click through to your site when they see you helping others. It's natural curiosity to want to find out more about the people who you see every day, and the best way to do that is to have a profile image of yourself. This is certainly better than some cartoon or other stock Gravatar or avatar next to your profile name. Images of "real" people instil trust, whereas hiding behind a stock image or logo does not. So remember to put a face to the name.

On your website they will see your picture again, and this further reinforces your perceived authority. The more people see your photo and read your contributions on these forums, the more they will recognize and respect you as an authority. This is a great way to build reputation, and it's nothing to do with the backlinks you can get from the forums, though these are useful as well.

Imagine how high your perceived authority will be when a visitor goes to several sites (in your niche) and sees you on all of them, answering questions and providing valuable information to others.

YouTube & Other Video Sites

Creating videos that offer valuable information in your niche is a great way to increase authority and "social proof" (especially when your photo or brand image appears in the video).

Videos that you create do not need to be 10 or 15 minutes long. You can easily create short two or three minute videos that discuss issues briefly in your niche. Video descriptions can be quite long, and they can **include a link back to your site**. If there is a relevant internal page on your site that makes the most sense to link to, do that, otherwise just link to your homepage. At the end of this book there is a bonus chapter on YouTube optimization.

YouTube allows you to create a video channel, which lists all of your videos in one place. Your YouTube profile can even have a link back to your site, and other sites that are part of your network like Twitter, Facebook, and Google+ etc. If someone likes one your videos, they can check out your channel to see what other videos you've created. They may even follow you on social media, post your videos to their own social networks, and/or visit your website.

There are a lot of other video sharing sites as well as YouTube, which also allow you to have a profile page. Try to use the same photo that you have on your main site and are using for your Gravatar. We are trying to build up the recognition factor here, so that people can automatically recognize you and think, "Oh yes I remember this expert."

Twitter

You can use twitter to include a brand photo and link back to your main site. As you add tweets, your photo goes through the twitter system and ends up again in front of people that have subscribed to your twitter feed. Even if you don't have many followers, your twitter page will have links back to your main site, which adds further authority to your persona.

There are a number of WordPress plugins available which automatically send a tweet for each new post published on your site. I wouldn't rely totally on these types of plug-ins for Twitter "content". The reason for this is because it's important to tweet interesting information that you find on a day-to-day basis, on other websites. A Twitter account that only sends tweets with links pointing to the owner's website is a spammy Twitter account.

Facebook Page

Another way that you can increase your authority is by setting up a Facebook page for your site or your business.

Facebook only allows you to have a single Facebook account. One of the biggest concerns I hear from my students is that they don't always want their friends and/or family to be aware of their business posts on Facebook.

Don't worry. If you set up a Facebook page for your website, it is totally separate from your personal profile account. You need a personal Facebook account to setup a Facebook page, but that's as far as the association goes. You can post specifically to your website Facebook page, and none of your friends or followers will even know it exists, unless you tell them about it of course. You can have multiple Facebook pages if you like, promoting different websites or products. When you login to Facebook, you will see direct links to your pages in the side column of your personal Facebook account, but these are not visible to your follows.

Web 2.0 "Blogs"

There are a number of websites which allow you to set up blogs on their own domain. Examples include WordPress.com, Blogger.com (owned by Google), Tumblr.com, and LiveJournal to name just a few. You simply go to their sites, sign up, and begin posting to your new blogs.

As you add more and more content to these blogs they become increasingly powerful, especially when you build backlinks from them.

Since you add the blog content yourself, you can insert links into that content, but don't overdo it. These blogs should add value and be high quality, just like every other type of backlink we are looking to build. I recommend you create small blogs with just 5-10 pages of great content related to your main site. Then add a single backlink to your main site from the homepage of the mini-site. That's right. Each of these mini-sites will contain just ONE link to your main site. Make your link the only external link on the homepage. On the other pages in the mini-site, link out naturally to authority sites within your niche. Use different types of content and make the mini-sites look natural.

RSS Feeds

If you use WordPress to build your site, then you already have an RSS feed for it. An RSS feed contains all of the most recent posts in a single file. You also get to define how many posts show in the feed from within the WordPress Dashboard.

You can find the feed by adding "/feed" to the end of your URL (without the quotes obviously).

For example:

http://ezseonews.com/feed/

Once you have your feed URL, you can then submit that feed to a number of different RSS Feed websites.

Every time you add new content to your site, the feed updates on these sites automatically, and you get a link back to the new content.

I don't believe that this type of link helps too much with ranking of pages, especially as posts will eventually slide off the bottom of the feed, but it does help to get new content indexed quickly by the search engines.

I would recommend submitting your feed to only two or three of the highest authority RSS directories that you can find.

I'd also recommend that you set up your feed to only display excerpts (and a maximum of 10 posts). This should keep you safe from the spammers who try to scrape content by stripping entire posts out of RSS feeds. And having only 10 posts in the feed is more of a safety precaution than anything else. After all, we don't want the last 100 posts hyperlinked on three different RSS feed directory sites. This would be overkill and look like we were trying to manipulate rankings.

Site Directories

Getting your site listed in directories is one of the oldest forms of back-linking. However, directory listings don't give you much by way of a ranking boost, if anything at all. There are also a number of directories you should NOT submit your site to, namely low quality or niche directories unrelated to your own site.

There are software programs that can submit your site to multiple directories, but I would suggest you save your money and just handpick the most relevant ones (particularly the specialist niche directories that match your chosen niche), and then submit by hand. More is NOT better. Always look for fewer, quality submissions, where the submission site is a close match to your own. For example, if you have a Paleo diet site, look for directories that specialise in nutrition.

While these links won't help your rankings too much, they will help diversify your backlink profile, making it look more natural, and this is always a good thing.

Guest Blogging

Guest Blogging is a powerful way to get high quality links pointing to your site. It's kind of like *Article Marketing 2.0* where you submit articles to sites that accept "guest posts".

The big difference between guest posting and article directories is that guest blogs can be higher quality and much more related to your own niche. For example, you could find a lot of health-related blogs that would accept health related articles from you, but it would be harder to find article directories that were specifically health related.

Guest posting works like this:

There are sites out there that are looking for people to write content for them. You write a piece of content and submit it to these sites. If they like your article, they will post it on their website.

When you submit your guest article, you include a resource box that can contain links back to your website (or a link in the body of your article). You will need to check the terms and conditions of the sites you are writing for to see whether it's possible to include links within the body of the article. If you can do that, then make sure your links look authoritative, like we discussed earlier. Remember this?

> Curcumin has shown remarkable <u>anti-cancer properties</u> not only in stripping the cancer cells defenses to make them more visible to the body's natural immune system, but also in cell apoptosis.

That looks a lot spammier than this example:

> Curcumin has shown remarkable anti-cancer properties not only in stripping the cancer cells defenses to make them more visible to the body's natural immune system, but in an article "<u>Curcumin initiates cancer cells death</u>", the author describes experimental results showing cell apoptosis occurring.

The second one is also more Google-friendly as it is not using keyword anchor text. Instead, it uses the title of the article it links to, like a real reference.

Finding Guest Blogs

You can easily find sites that will accept your work by doing a Google search and entering the following:

"write for us" + KEYWORD

KEYWORD is obviously your main niche word or phrase.

e.g. "write for us" + health

This will return all of the websites that have the phrase "Write for Us" and are related to the health industry. Here are the top few Google results for that term at the time of writing:

NOTE: PageRank data displays in the actual SERPs using a free browser plugin called <u>SEO Quake</u>. This is available for Firefox, Chrome, Opera and Safari.

With guest blogging, you can pretty much guarantee getting your content onto high PR websites.

These sites can have a lot of authority in the eyes of Google, and are therefore excellent places to get your content published. However, there are other benefits too.

Not only do you get backlinks from an authority site, but you'll also get to post your photo and site URL, which further boosts your personal authority in the niche. For each article accepted there is a new audience, and one that your own site probably never gets. In this way, guest blogging is a great method to "piggy back" on other peoples traffic.

PDF Distribution

You can distribute PDF files, which contain links to your website, to a number of special PDF distribution sites. Again, each site you distribute the PDF file to can include your profile picture and link back to your own site. To create PDFs, you can use existing content or simply write new content for the file.

Microsoft Word or the free OpenOffice suite, both have built in features to convert text documents into PDF format.

One of the best-known examples of a site that you can upload PDF documents to is:

http://www.scribd.com/

You can find a lot of websites that accept PDF submissions by searching Google for "submit eBooks" or "submit PDF".

Again, like everything else, look for quality sites and think less about quantity.

Blog Commenting

Blog commenting is easy. Go to a blog post related to your own niche, and leave a comment with a link back to your own site.

Blog commenting has been heavily abused by spammers over the years, and gets a lot of bad press because of that. However, I've done some tests recently and found that they do still work when done properly. They won't give you a massive boost in rankings, but they will diversify your backlink profile (important).

For the perfect blog comment, look for a quality site in your niche that allows comments, and preferably does not use the "nofollow" attribute on comment links. If it does use "nofollow", don't let that put you off. Nofollow links may not count for much, but they are part of a natural link profile nonetheless, and should therefore be included as a part of your overall link building campaign. Don't forget too, that even a "nofollow" link can still send visitors (traffic) to your site when someone clicks on it.

To create a comment:

1. Read the article you are commenting on and also read other people's comments too.

2. Add a comment that interacts with the original author, or another commenter. The comment should add to the conversation on that page. Add something that the webmaster will want to approve.
3. When adding a comment, you'll have fields for "your name" and "website URL". If there is no website field, don't waste time leaving a comment. In the name field, add your real name (or the penname you use on your site), either first or full name is fine. Never add a keyword phrase in the name field. In the URL field, enter your website homepage URL.
4. Note that many webmasters will delete comments with URLs in the body. Never add links to the body of your comment, unless there is a good reason for doing so, i.e. answering someone's question.

Backlink Velocity

The speed at which you create backlinks to a site can raise a red flag with Google.

If you have a site that gets 10 visitors a day, for example, does it make sense if that site has 50+ backlinks to it in a single day? If doesn't add up if those backlinks were all obtained naturally (other people independently linking to your site because of the great content).

I would recommend starting very slowly with any new site. Remember too, that it is very important that the backlink profile to your site is diverse so that it looks natural. This means lots of different types of backlinks from a wide range of IP addresses.

My primary goal for any new site is to create **epic** content that will attract links, and to then share it with social media channels in the hope that it becomes popular and gets shared around.

After creating several pieces of quality content, in an attempt to attract links, I will then turn my attention to creating a few links of my own. First up, I'll look for broken link opportunities and try to get a few from sites related to my niche. Once I've exhausted those, I'll look at using my "re-purposed" backlink content to get backlinks from some of those other sources we mentioned earlier.

IMPORTANT! Make sure you build links slowly. A link or two every week is perfect for a new site. Once your visitors pick up, you can go a little faster, but in 2015, quality of backlinks is far more important than quantity; something I can't emphasise enough. In fact, quantity will actually work against you in the long-run if those links are low quality. This is because low-quality links are hardly "diverse", and therefore raise a red flag, indicating that someone is building those links in a cheap and underhanded manner.

When to Stop Back-linking

If you have the link-bait style of content we discussed at the beginning of this section, then your pages will attract links naturally. When this happens, you should concentrate on adding new, high quality content to keep your visitors happy and to attract new links.

If you don't have content that naturally attracts links, you will need to go out looking for backlinks, and I'd recommend you do so on a continuous basis.

As discussed earlier, I'd suggest using the title of the page you are linking to, or its bare URL, as the link text.

Avoid using keyword rich anchor text because there is a real danger of raising the over-optimization flag. Google may decide you have too many spammy links and penalise the site. If you want keyword-rich anchor texts pointing to a page on your site, then linking to it from other pages within the site is the best option, in fact it's encouraged.

As mentioned earlier, don't worry about trying to rank at the top of Google for specific keyword terms as this is old hat and no longer works. If your page deserves to rank at the top of the SERPs for a phrase, it will have more chance of doing so if you concentrate on building authority. Remember that Google knows what your page is about. They don't need over-optimized anchor text to tell them. If they think it's worthy of the #1 slot, they'll rank it at #1. If they don't, then work more on the quality/value of the content, along with the authority of your site/page. Also bear in mind that pages optimized for a keyword phrase (especially commercial keyword phrases) rarely rank well for that phrase.

Backlinks to Backlinks

Whenever you build a site you should be tracking a lot of information so that you can fine tune things when necessary. One of the most important things to track is the backlinks pointing to your project.

Majestic SEO is a good free tool to do just this. Once you have set up Majestic SEO, wait for the data to start coming in.

You will get a list of all the backlinks pointing to your site. Download the list (Majestic SEO allows you to download the list as a spreadsheet) and check them to make sure that the backlinks still exist/work. Delete any links from the list that no longer exist or work (highlighted). This way you only end up with a list of web pages that actively link to your site.

Work your way through the list, and create new backlinks to each of these backlinks. This is something called "link reinforcement".

You can use any method of back-linking you want to, but I would recommend you only point quality links at these backlinks. This obviously means more work on your behalf, but I'll explain why it's important a little later. The idea is to make each page linking to your page stronger, and therefore able to pass more link juice (authority) to your site.

Here it is as a diagram:

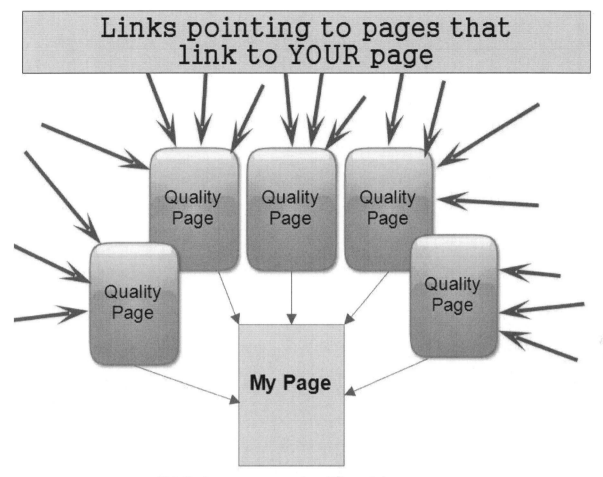

Links pointing to pages that link to YOUR page

Quality Page | Quality Page | Quality Page | Quality Page | Quality Page

My Page

BIG Increase in Rankings

In my opinion, many webmasters go wrong with this type of backlinks-to-backlink strategy. They often tend not worry about the quality of the backlinks to their backlinks. Instead they blast thousands of profile links, social bookmarks, spun articles, etc. at these backlinks in an attempt to boost them. It doesn't work.

Most webmasters who use this strategy assume that their site is safe, since these poor quality spammy links DO NOT point directly at their own site, but at the backlinks to their site (sites holding your backlinks are referred to as buffer sites or pages). Some webmasters assume that these buffer sites provide a type of immunity against penalties. They're wrong, of course.

Google hates linking schemes, and pyramid systems like this are no exception. Is it too farfetched to think that the negative SEO we saw earlier could render this type of link pyramid not only useless, but also harmful to your site? In the diagram above, if those links to your backlinks are good quality, you have nothing to worry about. However, what if those links pointing at your backlinks are low quality, spammy links? Let's re-draw that diagram.

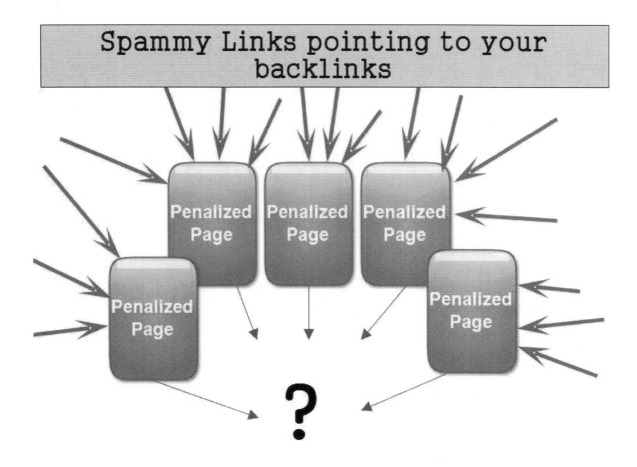

Now, instead of quality links pointing at the backlinks, we have poor quality, spammy links. These in turn penalize the pages that hold the links pointing directly your website. What happens now, as those pages link to your site, is that Google can follow the trail, and here's what happens.

Spammy Links pointing to your backlinks

Page gets a penalty and loses rankings

The penalty passes down the pyramid and your page is penalized as a consequence.

When Google decided to pass negative ranking factors through links (allowing negative SEO to work), it allowed penalties to pass down pyramid linking schemes, thus removing any immunity that was previously available through buffer sites.

A few years ago, everyone assumed that negative SEO was impossible, that is, if you wanted to take out your competition by pointing a lot of poor links at their site, it simply wouldn't work. Google even told us it wouldn't work. However, today we know this is no longer true. The reality is that poor-quality inbound links can hurt any webpage.

It makes sense though, doesn't it? I mean, *if* Google introduced a system where poor links pass on a negative ranking factor, then they would be wasting a massive opportunity to wipe out a lot of spammers if they didn't allow these penalties to trickle down the link pyramids.

So how do we stop someone else building spammy links to our pages in their attempts to get our site penalized? Well, the simple answer is we can't.

You may remember a recent report I mentioned earlier by MicrositeMasters.com. In that report they suggested that bad links were losing their ability to negatively affect site rankings. This was because Google were now simply ignoring them as opposed to applying penalties. If this is true, we can stop worrying so much about negative SEO and just concentrate on building high quality links. However, and just to make sure, I'd recommend you take a look at the Disavow tool. This is a tool Google gave us to help fight back against negative SEO. In giving us this tool, Google effectively said that all links to our website, good or bad, are our sole responsibility. Let's take a look at the Disavow tool and see how it works.

The Disavow Tool - How to Fix Bad Links to Your Site

Several years ago, webmasters were not held responsible for the links pointing to their own sites. Negative SEO just did not work, and Google themselves told us that bad links could not hurt a site's rankings.

In the last year or two things have changed. Google altered the rules so that bad backlinks *could* now hurt page (and site) rankings. However, because of the whole negative SEO angle, Google needed to provide a system to make webmasters truly accountable for the links to their sites, whether they had created them or not. In other words, if a website became the target of a negative SEO campaign, Google wanted the webmaster to fix it, and so the Disavow tool was born.

The Disavow tool allows webmasters to report bad links pointing at their sites, in the hope that Google will not count them as part of that site's backlink profile.

Therefore, if someone points a lot of spammy links at your site to try to get it penalized (wiped off the SERPs), Google gave you this tool so that you could use it to tell them about those links, and hopefully get them devalued to the point where they no longer contribute to your rankings.

Before we look at the Disavow tool in more detail, let me just state something: Just because we can report "bad" links to Google, it does not mean Google will listen to us or take action. Google have said that webmasters should use the Disavow tool as a last resort. The first step should always be to contact webmasters who are linking to you and ask them to remove the offending link(s). If those webmasters refuse to remove the links, or simply ignore your requests, then that is what the Disavow tool is for.

I should also mention that if Google do disavow links, it could take some time. One of my sites was the victim of negative SEO, and after disavowing those bad links, it took around six months for the site to recover. I recommend you constantly monitor the backlinks to your site (Google Webmaster Tools will show you the recent backlinks it has found), and disavow spammy links as you find them, that's if you can't get them removed by approaching the webmasters first.

Checking Your Link Profile & Creating a Disavow File

The first step in using the Disavow tool is to find the links that point to your site and evaluate them. You need to identify the links that may be causing your site harm. These links include:

1. Links on pages with scraped content.
2. Links on pages with spun content.
3. Links on pages with very poor/limited content (in terms of language, spelling, grammar, etc).
4. Links on sites that have been penalised in Google.
5. Links on irrelevant sites, or sites with dubious content.
6. Site-wide links that appear on all of the pages of a linking website.
7. Any link that you would not want Google to manually inspect.

Fortunately, Google Webmaster Tools provides us with an easy way to do a link audit. You need a free Webmaster Tools account for this, with your site linked to that account.

Assuming you have linked your website to your Webmaster Tools account, Google will list the backlinks to your project. It can take a while for these backlinks to start showing, so link up your site as soon as possible

To do this, login to Webmaster Tools and click on the site you want to inspect.

In the menu on the left side, select **Links to Your Site** from the **Search Traffic** menu.

On the right, you'll see a list of links to your site:

Links to Your Site

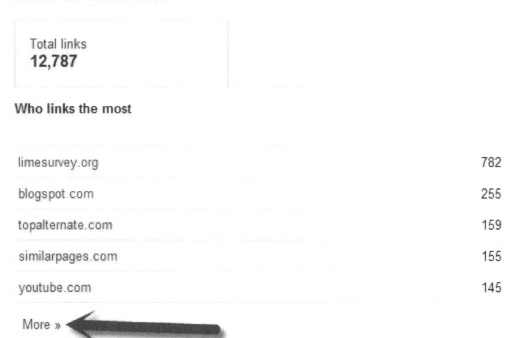

Total links
12,787

Who links the most

limesurvey.org	782
blogspot.com	255
topalternate.com	159
similarpages.com	155
youtube.com	145

More »

Google only shows you a few links by default, but if you look at the bottom of the list, you'll see a link to "**More**". Click it.

Overview » **All domains**
Top 480 domains that have links to pages on your site.

Download this table   Download more sample links   Download latest links

You now have a button to "**Download latest links**". Clicking this button will allow you to choose the format of the download.

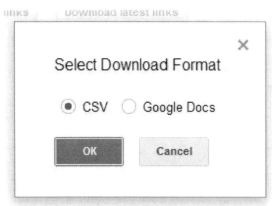

Select Download Format

⦿ CSV   ◯ Google Docs

OK   Cancel

The CSV format will download a spreadsheet that you can view in Excel or similar spreadsheet programs. Alternatively, you can download the file in Google Docs format.

If you don't use Google Docs, I recommend you give it a try. Just go to **docs.google.com**

You simply login to Google Docs with your Gmail email address and password.

Now if you select Google Docs from Webmaster Tools, and then click the OK button, the spreadsheet opens directly in Google Docs:

	A	B
1	Links	First discovered
2	http://www.limesurvey.org/en/home/69-limesurvey-news/general-news/1167-limesurvey-in-sri-lanka-plus-versions-and-the-comfortupdate-en-gb-4	11/25/2013
3	http://stuffgate.com/stuff/website/top-197000-sites	11/25/2013
4	http://domainprcheck.com/page/2024/?s=we	11/25/2013
5	http://contacts.pingerati.net/blogs/directory/business/sma 895/	11/25/2013
6	http://phpsurveyor.org/en/?start=42	11/24/2013
7	http://phpsurveyor.org/en/?start=126	11/24/2013
8	http://alexa.d-yn.com/?domain=ptgui.com	11/24/2013
9	https://www.limesurvey.org/en/home/69-limesurvey-news/general-news/1067-limesurvey-186-released-en-gb-4	11/23/2013

This spreadsheet will list all of the links Google wants you to know about.

Not only do you get the URL, but you also get the date that the link was first discovered. This means you can check all of the links the very first time you do a link audit. Then, in a month or two, you only need to check the new links that Google are reporting since your last check.

OK, so you need to work your way through the list of links and pull out any that you suspect are harming your website.

Google gives you two ways to deal with bad links. You can either report them on a link-by-link basis, or you can report a whole domain. If you report the domain, then the links are disavowed which point to your site. You can create a plain text file to use as your disavow list.

To disavow a single URL, just list the URLs, one on each line.

The format for reporting an entire domain is as follows:

Domain:somebaddomain.com

Google also encourages you to use comments in your disavow file. These comments can be for you, or for Google, outlining the steps you have carried out to get the links removed. For example, if you have tried contacting a webmaster to get links removed, and they have ignored your requests, you can include that information in a comment, before listing the appropriate URLs or domain.

To add comments, simply use the # symbol. A valid comment would look something like this:

 # Webmaster has ignored my request to remove these links.

If you want to write more, just go onto a second line, with the # at the start. For example:

Webmaster has not replied to my emails requesting link removal

Contacted on 16/08/2013, and again on 06/09/2013

Google provide the following example as a valid disavow file:

```
# example.com removed most links, but missed these
http://spam.example.com/stuff/comments.html
http://spam.example.com/stuff/paid-links.html
# Contacted owner of shadyseo.com on 7/1/2012 to
# ask for link removal but got no response
domain:shadyseo.com
```

In their example, the webmaster wants two URLs disavowed, plus all links on the shadyseo.com domain.

Once you have built up your disavow file, you need to upload it to Google. One thing I recommend you do is add the following comment to the beginning of the disavow file:

 # Last updated 10/10/2013

Save the file to your computer when you're done. The next time you want to do a link audit, you will know the date of your previous audit and can just look at the new links since that date (remember that Google gives us the date a link was found).

Uploading the disavow file to Google is simple.

Go to this URL:

https://www.google.com/webmasters/tools/disavow-links-main

You will need to login using your Webmaster Tools login details.

Select the website from the drop down list, and then click the Disavow button:

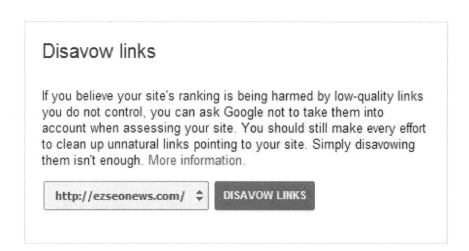

You will get a warning before you can upload the disavow file:

Disavow Links

This is an advanced feature and should only be used with
caution. If used incorrectly, this feature can potentially harm
your site's performance in Google's search results. We
recommend that you only disavow backlinks if you believe that
there are a considerable number of spammy, artificial, or low-
quality links pointing to your site, and if you are confident that
the links are causing issues for you.

Disavow Links

If you want to proceed, click the **Disavow Links** button.

Disavow Links

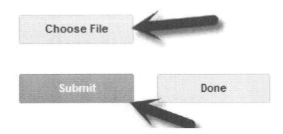

This is an advanced feature and should only be used with caution. If us
potentially harm your site's performance in Google's search results. W
disavow backlinks if you believe that there are a considerable number c
quality links pointing to your site, and if you are confident that the links

Upload a text file (*.txt) containing **only** the links you want to disavow.

Now you have a button to **Choose File**. Click that and select the disavow text file that you saved earlier.

Finally, click the **Submit** button to upload the file to Google.

Updating the Disavow File

When you need to update the disavow file, e.g. to include more URLs or domains, simply add the new URLs and domains to the file. Make sure you change the comment at the top to the current date so you can keep track. Once done, go back to the disavow tool and re-upload your updated file. Google only keep one file per site, so the last one you upload will be the file they use for any "disavowing".

I'd recommend you do a complete link audit on your site, and then recheck new links every month or two after that. Now that you are responsible for all links pointing to your site, you need to know who is linking to it, and whether those links are potentially harmful to your rankings. If they are, contact the webmaster and ask for their removal. Failing that, disavow them without hesitation.

I also want you to think about something else.

If there is a spammy web page linking to you, and you know that it can only be harmful to your rankings, it is possible that the site in question has more than one link to your site, even though you are not aware of them all. In cases like this, I always disavow the entire site rather than just the URLs. Think of it like this: if the page on that site is so bad that you want to disavow it, the chances are the whole site is pretty bad as well.

Future Alternatives to Link Building

Google is pretty good at detecting backlinks created for ranking purposes, and they are happy to slap any site that runs aggressive back-linking campaigns. So what does the future hold?

For the foreseeable future, backlinks will continue to be a major ranking factor, but there are other things you should start doing now.

Build Your Brand with Mentions

A "brand mention" is simply your "brand" mentioned in an article on another site. There is no physical backlink, just a mention of your brand.

There is a growing number of SEOs who think Google can actually recognise (and reward) brand mentions, associating the mention with the correct website. Quite often, your brand will be your domain name, so the more brandable your domain name, the more chance you have of Google correctly associating your brand-mention with your site.

For example, if your site is buycontactlensesonline.com, your domain is essentially a commercial keyword phrase that you have turned into an exact match domain (EMD). Any mention of "buy contact lenses online" on another site will not help your site, since your site is not a recognised brand.

However, if you named your site BetterVisionContacts.com, and your site had some authority, then another site mentioning "Better Vision Contacts" would probably work out as a brand mention in the eyes of Google.

SEOs think that brand mentions will form part of the ranking algorithm, if not now, then in the near future. They certainly already help build your authority, and authority, in the eyes of Google, is King.

The beauty of brand mentions is that this is a very safe way to get a ranking boost. Google won't be penalizing unlinked text any time soon. If you write guest posts for other websites, try inserting your brand into your article instead of a backlink.

Build Backlinks for Traffic Instead of Rankings, Using Nofollow

I mentioned previously that if you would build a backlink, even if Google did not exist, then it is natural in the eyes of Google. The reason is that you are not building it to improve your rankings; you are building it because it can benefit you in other ways.

A good example of why you might build a link, even if search engines did not exist, would be for click-through traffic. If you can get a link to your site on a high traffic web page, then the chances are that link would bring you some decent traffic since it's visible to a lot of eyeballs.

The only danger here is whether or not Google appreciate the reason for the link. Google might consider it a link to improve rankings, rather than a link for natural reasons. Don't worry. In cases like this, where your intent is to drive extra traffic from the webpage, you just nofollow that link. Google will then understand that the link is natural and not there to give you a ranking boost. It's always nice to get a boost in the rankings, but in this case, that's not why you placed the link on the page.

The temptation is there to never use nofollow tags on links, but it is becoming increasingly important to prevent penalties. It might all sound a bit too much right now, but I can promise you that once you get these things into your mind, you will intuitively know what to do in any given situation.

Summary of Backlinks

Just remember these simple guidelines when getting links:

1. Try to get links from as many different places as possible (we want IP diversity).

2. Look for quality rather than quantity. A handful of quality links will do more for your rankings than hundreds or thousands of spammy links (which could actually get your site penalized). Look for the "Holy Grail" backlinks by creating content other people want to link to.

3. Don't use keyword-rich anchor text in links you obtain from other websites. Always use your website title, URL, page URL or title of the page you are linking to as the anchor text.

4. Use internal linking (links that go from one page on your site to a different page on the same site.) to introduce keyword rich links to a page.

5. With links coming in from other websites, keep the percentage of keyword-rich anchor text to 5% or less.

6. Backlink to your backlinks to make them stronger, but only do this by using high quality links. By strengthening your backlinks like this, you'll need fewer of them to compete.

7. Carry out a link audit periodically on your site, and ask webmasters to remove any low quality, spammy links that may be affecting your rankings. Failing that, use Google's disavow tool.

4. What's in It for the Visitor?

You never get a second chance to make a first impression.

When a visitor arrives on your website, you have a very short time to make a good first impression. That first impression will decide whether they stay or go. So the first thing you need to do is make sure your site looks good. If you're using WordPress, then that's quite easy as there are many attractive WordPress designs out there to choose from.

Apart from the overall design, another aspect of your site, which will add to a good first impression, is the speed at which the page loads. This needs to be as fast as possible to avoid having visitors waiting for stuff. In fact, most visitors won't bother to stay if the page is still loading after just a few seconds.

Install Google Analytics and Get a Google Webmaster Tools Account

These two free tools can give you a huge amount of information on your site and its visitors. They are also Google's way to communicate with YOU. If there is anything Google is concerned about, they'll tell you about it in your Webmaster's account. They'll also notify you when your site is down or when there is a WordPress upgrade (if you use WordPress).

A lot of webmasters believe it's best to avoid these tools, thinking Google will use them against you, but I disagree. Google already have all the data they need on your site, and anyone who thinks otherwise is just deluding themselves. These two tools are a great way for Google to share that data with you.

Google's "Webmaster Tools" used to tell you how fast your site was loading and show you a graph of load times over a period of time. However, they have since retired this tool, but you can now find that information in Google Analytics instead.

A great alternative to checking your page load speed is to use an online tool like GTMetrix: http://gtmetrix.com/. You simply enter your page URL and GTMetrix will measure the load speed there and then, in real-time:

Report generated: Fri, Feb 22, 2013, 2:06 AM -0800
Test Server Region: Vancouver, Canada
Using: Firefox 14.0.1, Page Speed 1.12.9.1, YSlow 3.1.4

Looks like you're running WordPress
Have a look at our WP optimization tips »

Summary

| Page Speed Grade: (81%) ↕ | B | YSlow Grade: (76%) ↕ | C | Page load time: 2.63s Total page size: 916KB Total number of requests: 81 |

Not only do they give you the time in seconds for the page load, but they will also tell you which parts of your site are slowing things down, and what you can do to fix the problems.

Website Stickiness

In Google Analytics, Google will tell you the average time a visitor stays on your site, as well as the bounce rate (how quickly someone bounces back to Google search after visiting just a single page on your site).

Bounce rate and time on site are measures of how "Sticky" your site is.

Here is the bounce rate for one of my sites, taken at the time of writing:

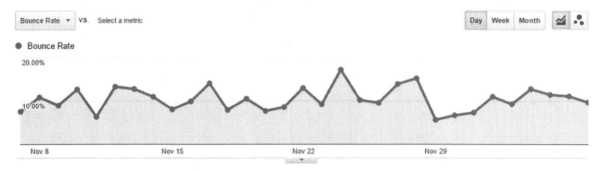

This is the average for the whole site.

You'll notice that the maximum bounce rate over the last month was less than 20%, with the average being around 10%. This means that only about 10% of people visiting my site go straight back to Google after reaching the landing page. Here are the averages for this site over the last month:

The average bounce rate of 10.32% and an average time on site of around 20 minutes is good. I'd say that this site was quite sticky, wouldn't you?

While that data is for the site as a whole, you can examine these metrics for individual pages too. This is good because it lets you see where your site is being let down. The idea is to find the content that does not hold your visitor's attention, and then fix it.

The next screenshot shows the data for a number of URLs on my site.

Avg. Time on Page	En.	Bounce Rate
00:20:04 Site Avg: 00:20:04 (0.00%)	?8 (98)	10.32% Site Avg: 10.32% (0.00%)
00:54:04	)	6.98%
00:05:23	1? ,)	31.90%
01:08:36	18 ⁄ₒ)	4.85%
01:20:36	%)	4.93%
00:06:14	⁄ₒ)	10.27%
00:17:28	%)	8.18%
01:20:31	)	5.31%
01:10:07		16.00%
01:09:19		7.45%
00:02:48	~%)	0.00%

Just look for the pages with the lowest "Avg. Time on Page" (left column) and the highest "Bounce Rate" (right column) and see if there is something you can do about those pages to improve their content and make them sticker. Any page with a high bounce rate is a clear indicator that it is not giving the visitor the "experience" they were looking for.

This book has already covered some of what's in this chapter. Even so, it is nice to have all of these ideas in one place, for easier reference as you work on your site. Let's look at the key ideas to bear in mind as you work on your website.

Important Aspects of a Web Page

You need to capture your visitor's attention and let them know what you have in store for them.

In terms of articles on your website, this can mean an eye-catching headline that makes them want to read more. If your visitor reads the headline and finds it interesting, they'll more than likely go on to read the opening paragraph. The first paragraph is almost as vital as the headline itself, so you might like to try creating an opening paragraph as a summary of what your visitor will find further down the page. Tell them what goodies lie in wait for them if they keep reading.

As you write content, try to keep sentences short (20-25 words). For paragraphs, look at four or five sentences each wherever possible. People hate large blocks of text, but they also hate sentences that are too long because they can become confusing and difficult to read. When you have finished writing your content, read it aloud to yourself. If you find any part(s) that need rereading to fully understand them, then something needs fixing. Similarly, if you find yourself hesitating over a word or sentence, something is interrupting the flow, so fix that too.

To make your articles easier to read, use sub-headings and bullet points. Pictures and diagrams can also help break up blocks of text, making the piece easier on the eyes for your visitor. Like that old adage goes: "A picture is worth a thousand words." It's true too, providing the image catches the reader's attention of course.

NOTE: Use ALT tags on images, but do not stuff them with keywords. Simply use an ALT tag that describes the image clearly.

Another important point is to use colours and fonts wisely. Don't put white fonts on black background or any other combination that causes eyestrain. Black font, or charcoal grey, on a white background is the best. Also, use fonts which work well online, like Verdana, Trebuchet and Georgia.

If you want to see some truly shocking usage of colours on the web, search Google images for the term **bad website design**.

While we're on the subject of content, be aware that people are a lot less patient than they used to be: http://news.bbc.co.uk/2/hi/technology/7417496.stm.

Be concise and to the point. Don't waffle just to get the word count higher because it won't keep your visitors around for very long.

To make your site sticky, you need to give your visitors what they want. That's it, in a nutshell! In order to do this, you need to know your visitor. Ask yourself the following questions:

- Who is it?
- What do they want?
- What answers to they need?
- What do they want to ask me?

Your homepage should guide the visitor quickly and easily to the section of your website that is of interest to them. Your visitor should be able to find what they need swiftly and effortlessly. Needless to say, a search box is essential for this purpose. Fortunately, adding a search facility is easy with WordPress ;)

Ways to Build Trust

1. The Mugshot: Include a photo of yourself in a prominent position on your website. The sidebars or in the logo are a good place for this. A photo helps build trust because the visitor can see who they are interacting with. Putting a face to the name is always a good thing when it comes to building an online reputation.

2. Create a Gravatar: If you use your photo as a Gravatar, then every time you post comments on other websites, your photo will appear automatically next to your comments. This goes back to what we were saying in the section on building authority. How much better is it for a visitor to arrive on your site and recognize your face? This can really help towards building a high level of trust.

3. Fresh content rules: If people arrive at your site and see that the content is several years old, this may be enough for them to click the back button. Keep stuff like reviews up to date. If you update a review, change the timestamp of the post in WordPress to reflect the new date. If the content is "ageless", consider removing the date/time stamp from the post.

4. Visible links to: A Privacy Policy, Terms of Use, and a Contact Us page are great ways to help build trust. On your contact page, you should ideally have

a real address as this helps further with the trust building. Again, it's a good idea to have your photo on the Contact Us page as well.

5. Create an About Us page: Here you can mention who you are and what your goals are for the site. On many websites, this is often one of the highest traffic pages, so don't be afraid to insert a signup box if you have a newsletter or short course to offer.

Types of Content Your Visitors Want:

1. Answer "real" questions on your pages: You can find the questions that people ask in your niche by looking at sites like Yahoo Answers, Quora and even Ask.com. Find real questions and create a Q&A section on your site using those questions. You can use the **site:** operator at Google to search for information on specific sites. Here is an example where I am searching Google for questions about juicing Vs blending at Quora.com:

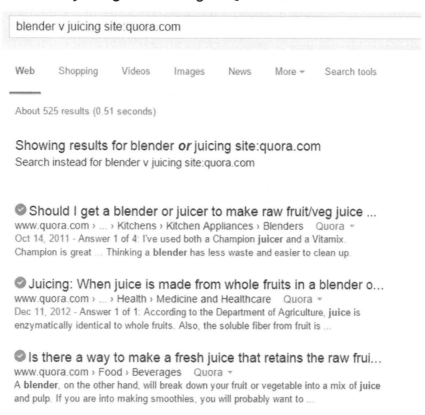

I am sure you can see how easy it is to find relevant, on-topic questions to use as the basis for your website content.

2. Buyer Guides: For example, if your site is about Android Tablets, give your visitors a free PDF that tells them what they need to know when it comes to buying one of these devices. You can use that free guide to build a list if you want to, by making visitors opt-in to your list before they get the free download URL.

3. Tutorials: Provide helpful tutorials for your visitors if you can think of some that are relevant to your niche.
4. Videos: Create informative, relevant videos and embed them in your web pages. Put a great title above the video to entice your visitor's to watch it. Never have your vids start automatically, always give visitors that option. Make sure the video content lives up to the title. Upload videos to Youtube.com and develop your own YouTube channel in your chosen niche. This will not only bring you extra traffic, but it will also build credibility and trust. You can link to this YouTube channel from your website.
5. Terminology Page: One type of page I usually include on my niche sites is a Terminology Page. A niche has its own vocabulary as we have seen, and often people want to know what certain words or phrases mean. A Terminology Page serves this purpose.

When creating new content, or looking for new ideas, ask yourself this question:

"What valuable information or resources can I offer that are not available on the top 10 sites in Google?"

Make Your Site Interactive

1. Allow Comments from visitors at the end of your articles. Invite or encourage your visitors to use the comments box. It's amazing how simple it is to say something along the lines of: "Hey, if you've got a question or an opinion on this, leave a comment at the bottom of this post". A lot of people don't bother, but it's a really effective call-to-action.

   Fulltime blogger Darren Rowse, once wrote a nice article on getting your visitors to comment: http://www.problogger.net/archives/2006/10/12/10-techniques-to-get-more-comments-on-your-blog/

   A lot of webmasters turn comments off on their site because of the huge amounts of spam they receive. However, by using a good spam blocker like Akismet (commercial) or the WordPress "Stop Spammers" plugin (an aggressive anti-spam plugin that eliminates comment spam): https://wordpress.org/plugins/stop-spammer-registrations-plugin/, you can eliminate 99% of all spam.

   Comments allow your visitor to interact with YOU, as well as with other commenters. If a visitor asks a question, make sure you always answer it. This starts a dialogue with your target audience and builds trust and authority. Visitors like to see that you're actually answering questions personally. Answering questions brings visitors back to your site, especially if you have a plug-in installed that allows them to track responses to their own comments (recommended).
2. By using a ratings and review plug-in (search the WordPress plugin directory), you can give your visitors the chance to award products their own star rating

when they leave a comment.

3. Polls are a great way to get your visitors involved. They allow visitors to express their opinion by a casting a quick vote. There are a few free polling scripts around to choose from.

4. Provide Social Media Icons after each post so that people can spread the word on your great content. There are a number of free plugins available. I recommend you try a few of these out to see which one works best with your site and its theme.

5. Add a forum. Forums can have quite an issue with spam at times, and that means they take a bit of maintaining. Even so, if you have time to run a forum, just know that these discussion boards can be a great way for people to interact with you and others, but they may take a while to generate visitors and members. Several WordPress plugins are available that will add a fully functional forum on your site.

BONUS Chapter - YouTube SEO

YouTube is owned by the search engine giant Google. Even if you didn't know that, you might have guessed there was a close relationship by looking at how many YouTube videos rank in the top 10 of Google search. YouTube videos that are ranked in the top 10 probably get quite good click through rates (CTR), simply because they have a thumbnail image of the video displayed in the SERPs. Sometimes, they even have a full sized video taking up the top slot.

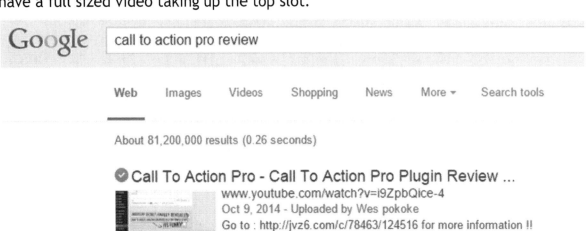

There are two videos for the above search phrases, ranked #1 and #2 on Google.

YouTube is also a major search engine in its own right. There are many people who use the search box on YouTube to find what they are looking for, thus bypassing Google search completely. However, just because Google own YouTube, that does not mean the ranking algorithms on YouTube and Google are the same. Look at this search on YouTube and then Google Search for the same phrase:

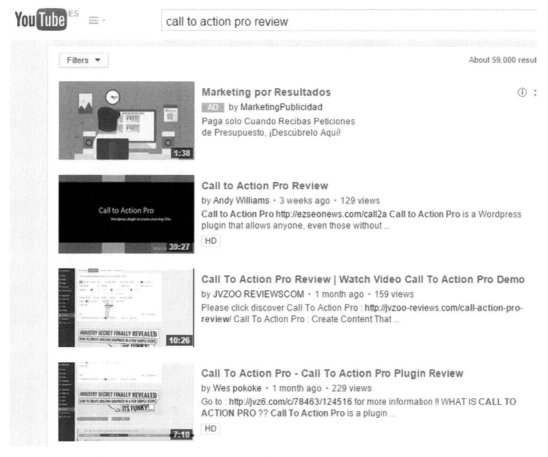

The video ranked #1 on Google is ranked #4 on YouTube.

The video ranked #2 on Google is ranked #12 on YouTube.

We've already seen that the ranking algorithm for Google is very complex, involving hundreds of different signals, both on page, and off.

YouTube's ranking is not as complex as Google Search, or at least it does not appear to be.

On YouTube, it is possible to rank a video using just on-page factors in less competitive niches. For example, in that screenshot above, my video is #1 (the top video (above mine) is a paid advert, so I'm not including that). If I search for that term in quotes, YouTube tells me that there are 185 videos using that exact phrase somewhere on the page. Therefore, with only around 185 direct competitors, I can easily rank #1.

The ease of ranking on YouTube in low competition niches has gotten some marketers excited, and here's why: By finding low competition phrases, and with good search volume, they can rank high on YouTube and get easy traffic to their sites. It sounds great, but let me burst that bubble. Ranking on YouTube is fine, but it's not the best. You really want your video ranking in the Google SERPs. That is where the majority of traffic will come from, not from the YouTube search results.

Let me give you an example.

Here is a search phrase that I found in Google Keyword Planner:

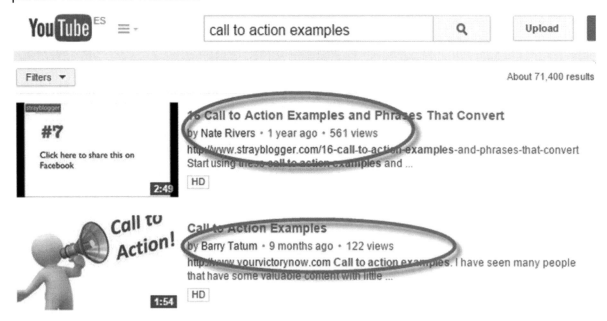

Ad group ideas	Keyword ideas		
Search terms		▼ Avg. monthly searches ?	Co
call to action examples		∠ 3,600	Lov

That screenshot tells me that this phrase is searched for 3,600 times a month.

OK, the first thing to do is see how many videos are actually optimized for that exact phrase.

A search on YouTube, using quotes, tells me 338 videos use that exact phrase on the page.

An intitle: "call to action examples" search tells me that only 11 videos use that exact phrase in the actual title. This is often a good indicator of how many videos have been optimized for a phrase.

It's probably going to be easy to rank at the top of YouTube with just on-page factor.

If you could rank #1 in YouTube for that phrase, how much traffic would it bring?

Well, Google Keyword Planner tells us that the phrase is searched for 116 times a day.

Let's now go over to YouTube and see how many times the top videos ranking for that phrase have been watched:

The number #1 ranked video has been watched 561 times in the 20 months since it was published. I know the YouTube screenshot says it is a year old, but if you click through to the video, you can see it was published much earlier than that.

This means the video's had around 28 views per month, on average.

The video in position #2 on YouTube has been seen 14 times per month.

So what happened to the 3,600 searches a month?

Well, there are two problems with using search volume reported by Google Keyword Planner.

1. The search volume is for Google, not YouTube.
2. The search volume is not very accurate.

For a video on YouTube to get decent traffic, it needs either a lot of search traffic ON YouTube, or the video needs to rank for the keyword phrase in Google Search, in the top 10, and preferably near the top of page one.

For any search phrase, if there are videos in the top 10 search results on Google, that's a good sign. However, to make sure people are really using those search phrases, check how many times those videos are watched on a monthly basis.

Before you spend time creating a video for YouTube, with the sole purpose of bringing in more traffic, ask yourself this: "Are there YouTube videos in the top 10 for this phrase, and how many views per month do those videos get?"

YouTube Video Optimization

This really is a two-part process.

1. Get the on-page factors right.
2. Build backlinks to the video from the best sources you can find.

These two steps will allow your video to rank near or at the top in YouTube, but also have a chance of ranking in Google's top 10 (assuming Google usually shows at least one video in the SERPs for that phrase).

Let's consider the on-page factors for YouTube videos.

The on-page SEO is much more like the Google SEO of old. Keywords are still King here, and spamming does work. I would, however, caution against creating spammy video titles or descriptions. It is only a matter of time before Google crack the YouTube whip and start to change things. In fact, the YouTube results are so spammy in some niches, that I am surprised Google hasn't already dealt with the problem.

OK, here is a checklist of on-page optimization that you can use to optimize your video for a specific phrase.

1. Add the keyword phrase in the video title. Put the phrase at the start, and try to make the title as short as possible.
2. Use your main keyword phrase in the video's filename.
3. Think of the description in the same way as you would think of a short article for your site. This will give it more chance of ranking in Google. Create a well-

themed description that uses the main keyword phrase in the first sentence, plus all of the important niche vocabulary further down. Include a link back to your website as a bare URL.

4. You need to add some tags to your submission. Make sure your main keyword is the first one. Include variations on that main keyword in the tags, and any other important niche vocabulary.

5. If you get comments on your videos, moderate them. Remove any spammy comments and reply to any questions you get. Engage with the people who leave comments.

6. Embed the video in a page on your own website, and provide some kind of commentary (as text) to accompany the video (a video on its own is scraped content even if you created it yourself). I often write longer articles and create a video to cover one aspect. The video then becomes a small unique part of the web page content rather than the dominant feature.

7. If your videos have a lot of speech, you might consider looking into the closed caption features provided by YouTube. YouTube will try to transcribe your video automatically for you, and it's not always good, but you can download the file and correct it. If you do this, you can then use the corrected transcription on your own site to accompany the video.

That's all there is to on-page optimization for YouTube videos.

After uploading your video, I recommend you use the social sharing buttons and share it to all of your social media channels. These will count as backlinks, albeit weak ones, but they give your video a chance to spread through social channels, if it's good enough.

Things Not to Do with YouTube

There are a lot of services out there that promise to help you with your YouTube promotions. The popular ones offer:

1. To send visitors to your video, boosting the number of views.
2. To provide your video with a gazillion "Likes".
3. To give you subscribers to your channel.

My advice is DO NOT use any services that artificially inflates the metrics of your video, not even if they say they are "real" people. They won't be, by the way.

YouTube remains one of the safest forms of backlinks to your site, so use them for that, as well as driving traffic to your site through links in the description. You can even monetize your YouTube videos with AdSense if you want to, so look into that if it's something that interests you. A video that goes viral with advertising on it can give you an unexpected and welcome windfall.

Part 2 - The SEO Checklist

Why Part 2?

The first part of this book is an overall White Hat strategy for SEO. However, for many of my students and clients, the biggest problem is where to start on an existing site that has lost its rankings. Most of us have been there. Everything was going really well, and then you wake up one day to find your Google traffic wiped out. Your question then becomes, "What the heck do I do now?"

This section will take you by the hand and guide you through a complete checklist of things you should objectively critique/fix on your website. Before I go on, I need to point out that a lot of people are not very objective about their own work. It's often hard to take criticism from other people and even harder to admit that you made a mistake somewhere along the way. However, for this process to work, you need to step outside of yourself. It's time to try to view your website differently, as a complete stranger might view it after arriving at your pages for the first time.

I'd also like to say that although you do need to be constructively critical, I don't want you to be too hard on yourself. Nearly everyone I know lost a site or two in the Google updates of the last few years, myself included. When Google first moved the goalposts, it caught a lot of people out, and I do mean a lot of people.

Pre-Panda and pre-Penguin, Google tolerated certain activities. Post-Panda and post-Penguin, they don't. As a result, they are now enforcing their Webmaster Guidelines, something that SEOs never really believed Google would do, but they did. It's Google's change in tolerance that got so many of us into trouble.

Let me give you an example of their "moving of the goal posts".

We have known for some time that Google doesn't like us building backlinks to our sites, especially with automated tools. How did we know? Google told us. So why did so many people engage in link-building campaigns using automated tools that created hundreds or thousands of low quality links in a short space of time? The answer is simple. At that time, Google tolerated this behaviour; in fact they even rewarded it. When you see your competitor building all these links and jumping ahead of you in the search engine results, it's only natural that you want to do the same to get your rankings back, so that's what many of us did.

As long as Google tolerated (and rewarded) aggressive link-building, people continued to do it. Google knew that.

Google Panda, and probably more specifically, Google Penguin, changed all of this. Google went from being a very tolerant search engine, to one of zero tolerance, overnight!

For as long as I can remember, Google has published Webmaster Guidelines to tell us what they consider acceptable and what is not. Before Panda and Penguin, these guidelines were simply that - **guidelines**. Most of use chose to ignore them because we had no choice. If we followed their guidelines, then we could not rank above our competitors who did not. However, with the arrival of Panda and Penguin, these guidelines became **strict rules**, and rules that had to be followed or else.

All of the previously tolerated "illicit" activities, like link building, were suddenly a big problem for the websites that employed those activities. Webmasters who held the number one spot for years, suddenly found their site gone from page one. Many sites were gone from the Google SERPs altogether.

The reason why so many websites lost their rankings overnight was simply because those sites had not followed the guidelines in the past.

I wrote this section of the book to help you more easily identify and fix the problems you may have with your website. I use the same checklist on my own websites, and those of my students and clients, so I know it works when followed tightly.

What Does Google Want?

Before we start the checklist, I thought it would be a good idea to have a quick reminder of what it is that Google actually wants. You can read their guidelines for yourself, here:

http://support.google.com/webmasters/bin/answer.py?hl=en&answer=35769

Near the top of that page, it says:

> *"Even if you choose not to implement any of these suggestions, we strongly encourage you to pay very close attention to the "Quality Guidelines," which outline some of the illicit practices that may lead to a site being removed entirely from the Google index or otherwise impacted by an algorithmic or manual spam action."*

It is important that you take this statement seriously. Google will remove or penalize your site if they catch you carrying out any activities they don't approve of. Unlike the rhetoric of the past, Google actually means what it says these days.

There are a lot of webmasters out there who resent Google's attempts to stifle their SEO "creativity", and I often hear people say things like, "Who cares what Google want..." usually followed by "I'll do whatever I want with my own site. Stuff Google!" This is all fine if you know the risks and can accept the consequences. At the end of the day, this is Google's search engine and they can do what they want with it. The bottom line is this: if you want free traffic from Google, then you need to follow their guidelines.

Please understand that you can no longer walk the black or grey hat path and stay under Google's spam radar. Read this:

Reporting spam

We're constantly working to improve the quality of our search results. If you've found a particular site that's spamming our index, we'd like to hear about it. To learn about what we consider acceptable practices, please see our Webmaster Guidelines.

The best way to tell us about a site that doesn't meet our guidelines is by submitting a Spam Report at https://www.google.com/webmasters/tools/spamreport?hl=en. You can also tell us about spam in rich snippets. Spam Reports are submitted directly to our engineers and are used to devise scalable solutions to fight spam.

We appreciate your assistance in maintaining the quality of our search results.

That link to submitting a spam report opens up the following page (after you login to Google Webmaster Tools):

Google

Search Console

"Webspam" refers to pages that try to trick Google into ranking them highly. Before you file a webspam report, see if the page might have a different problem:

Paid links

This page is selling or buying links.

Copyright and other legal issues
This page should be removed under applicable law.

Objectionable content

This page is inappropriate.

Personal/private
This page discloses private information.

Malware

This page is infected.

Phishing
This page is trying to get sensitive information.

Other Google products
This page abuses Google products other than Search, e.g., AdSense, Google Maps, etc.

Rich Snippets
This page doesn't comply with Google's rich snippets guidelines.

Something else is wrong
This page has other, non-webspam related issues.

This page is really webspam. [Report webspam]

This page makes it easy for your competitors to report your pages if you are using "Webspam" techniques to rank in the SERPs.

Black and grey hat SEOs not only have to keep under Google's radar, they also have to keep under the radar of their competitors who will be quick to report them. With so much profit in ranking on page one of the Google SERPs, any new web page that pushes out established sites from the top 10 slots will most certainly come under heavy scrutiny.

What to Avoid

According to the Webmaster Guidelines, here are some things you definitely need to avoid.

- **Pages designed for the search engines, not the visitor**. We've all seen these in the search engine results pages (SERPs). They are the pages designed with the sole purpose of ranking well in Google, without any thought given to what the visitor might think when they arrive at the site. Google want engaging, unique content (and I'm talking unique in terms of "voice", discussion or ideas, not just the words and their order on the page).
- Any **trick** or "**loophole**" designed to help a web page rank higher in the search engine. That pretty much covers most of the SEO pre-2012.
- **Content that is auto-created using a software tool**. Most content-generating software produces gibberish, so this is an obvious point. Even if it's not gibberish, it won't be the valuable, coherent, unique content that Google want to see. One type of tool that deserves special attention is the article spinner. Spinners can produce hundreds of near perfect "unique" articles in just a few minutes in the hands of an expert. Many people have used these spun articles extensively in back-linking campaigns. Well, Google won't tolerate spun content anymore, whether it's on your site or used in backlinks to your site.

   Other examples of auto-generated content include articles translated by software (badly) without a human review, scraped content from RSS feeds, and "stitching or combining content from different web pages without adding sufficient value." This last point should be of interest to content curators who don't **add sufficient value** to the content they curate.

- "**Linking schemes**" **that are designed to manipulate rankings in the search engine**. Wow! That's a big one. Google have told us that they don't want us building links to our site for the sole purpose of better rankings. Back-linking is one of the most effective ways to improve your rank in Google, so obviously we all still do it. Just by linking two or more of your own sites together can be considered a "linking scheme" if the sole point is to help those sites rank better. Other things Google don't like are sites which buy or sell links to pass on PageRank (PR). They also don't like reciprocal linking between sites, or websites that have used automated tools to build backlinks. Google don't even like text links inserted into the body of articles, your "guest post" on other websites, if those links are simply there to manipulate your web page rankings.
- **Websites that serve up one version of a page to the search engines, yet a different page to the visitors.** This is what we call "cloaking". Webmasters use this to try and trick the search engines into ranking the "sales" page higher. The page the search engines see is keyword rich (helping it to rank), whereas the version the visitor sees is completely different.
   "Sneaky redirects" are similar to cloaking and often achieved with JavaScript

(computer programming language commonly used to create interactive effects within web browsers) or a Meta refresh (a method of instructing a web browser to automatically refresh the current web page). The result is that the page the visitor sees is not the same page that the search engine spider crawled and ultimately ranked for in Google.

- **Pages that have "hidden" text**. In other words, text that is invisible to the visitor. This is achieved using CSS to make the text the same colour as the background. Visitors don't see the text but the search engines do, since they crawl and read the text based document.
- **Websites that use "doorway pages"**. These are poor quality pages, designed to rank for a single keyword or key phrase. Sites that use doorway pages often have hundreds or thousands of them. Their sole purpose is to rank high for a single search term and deliver visitors from the search engine.
  As an example, think of a double glazing company that wants to rank in every state of the United States for the term "double-glazing Utah" (or whatever state a person is searching from). One way this has been done in the past is to create a generic webpage optimized for "double-glazing Utah" and then duplicate it, swapping out the word "Utah" for "Texas" and then repeating the process for every state. That's 50 pages of "duplicate content", in Google's eyes. That same site might identify 99 other keyword phrases they want to rank for besides the obvious "double-glazing". If they create doorway pages for each state, with all of the phrases they want to rank for, the site would end up with 5,000 pages of duplicate spam.
- **Affiliate websites that don't add enough value**. These include the typical Amazon affiliate website where each page is a single review of a product that links back to the Amazon store via an affiliate link. In many of the poorer sites, the review content contains nothing that isn't already on Amazon or the manufacturers own website. Affiliate sites MUST add significant value.

Google Suggestions

- **Use clear, intuitive navigation on your site with text links**. Every page on your site needs to be reachable from a link somewhere on the site. A sitemap helps here (Google recommends you have one), but it is also a good idea to interlink your content, providing that is, it helps the visitor navigate your site. We discussed navigation in the first section of this book.
- **Don't have too many links on any given page**. Sites like Wikipedia: http://www.wikipedia.org/, seem to ignore this rule, yet they still rank well for a huge number of searches. However, Google trusts and accepts Wikipedia as an authority website, so what's good for them may not necessarily be good for you and your site.
- **Websites that have useful, information-rich content**. Think here in terms of content written for the visitor, not for the search engine.
- **ALT tags that actually describe the image**. Be aware that ALT tags are often read to the visually impaired by text-to-speech software. That makes the ALT

tag an important source of information for people who cannot actually see the image, so use this tag to describe the image in a brief but accurate way.

- **Sites should not have broken links.** There is a good free software tool called Xenu Link Sleuth: http://home.snafu.de/tilman/xenulink.html. Link Sleuth spiders your site and checks for broken links for you, so there really is no excuse.

OK, I'm sure by now you get the general idea.

We'll look at some of the other things Google like and don't like as we work our way through the checklist.

THE SEO CHECKLIST

Use this checklist to identify problems on a website.

There is a summary of the checklist at the end of this section.

Checklist Point #1 - the Domain Name

Exact Match Domains

In the past, keywords in your domain name helped your website to rank for those keywords. The ultimate ranking boost was from something called an Exact Match Domain, or EMD for short. An EMD took keyword "stuffing" to the extreme, by making the domain name identical to the main keyword phrase you were trying to target.

For example, if you wanted to rank well for "buy prescription drugs online", then the exact match domain would be buyprescriptiondrugsonline.XXX where XXX is any one of the top-level domains (TLD), i.e .com, .net, .org, etc. By merely having that exact key phrase in the domain name gave you an unfair ranking advantage for that phrase. SEOs soon spotted this and EMDs became hot favourites for anyone trying to make quick money online.

On September 28, 2012, Matt Cutts (head of Google's webspam team) tweeted the following:

Google had finally decided to take action on "low-quality" EMDs and prevent them from ranking, simply because of the phrase in the domain name.

Now, if you have an EMD, don't panic. Google's algorithm targets **low quality EMDs** from the search results, not good sites that happen to be on an EMD. Having said that, there is often some collateral damage with big changes to the algorithm updates, so it's inevitable that a few good sites get hit at times. You need to decide if your site is a quality EMD or a low quality one, before deciding to keep it or not.

The first thing I recommend you look at when evaluating the quality of an EMD, is whether it is a commercial phrase. If it is, then there may be no hope for your site unless the phrase is your actual brand.

As an example, here are the estimated costs per click for some contact lens related phrases as reported by Google's keyword tool.

☐	**contact lenses** online order ▾	€5.96
☐	**contacts lenses** online ▾	€5.65
☐	buy **contact lenses** on line ▾	€5.60
☐	ordering **contact lenses** online ▾	€5.56
☐	order **contacts lenses** online ▾	€5.55
☐	order contacts online ▾	€5.52
☐	online contacts lenses ▾	€5.52

Any of those phrases turned into an EMD would be suspect. It would be hard to convince Google that your site was quality if you used any of those commercial terms as your domain name.

Google's update eliminated the power of EMDs, meaning webmasters stopped using them, or at least webmasters who understood SEO did. Take that first phrase as an example. The EMD would be:

contactlensesonlineorder.com

Surely someone would have registered that in the past to take advantage of the EMD ranking power. If they could rank for that phrase and stick AdSense ads on the site, then they'd be making a good chunk of change every time someone clicked on an advert.

When typing that domain into my web browser, this is what I get:

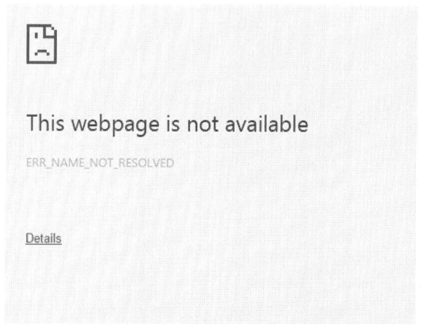

However, if I search using the Way Back Machine: http://web.archive.org, which looks for archived versions of websites, this is what I see:

That site existed in 2009, and then again in 2011.

Using Way Back Machine, I can even look at that site as it appeared back in 2009 or 2011. Here it is in 2009:

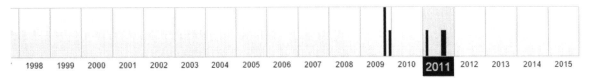

Contact Lenses Online Order

Save up to 70% off retail contact lens prices. Fast, Simple and Cheap.

- Acuvue
- Biomedics
- Freshlook
- Soflens
- Proclear

We carry all popular brands of contact lenses including Acuvue, Biomedics, Focus, Freshlook, Soflens, Purevision prices.

Best Seller Contact Lenses

Focus Dailies Toric - 90 Pack Contact Lenses (90 lenses) $64.95

Biofinity Toric C

Notice the main header on the page uses the exact same phrase. This is a typical example of a low quality EMD.

So, why is that EMD no longer an active site?

The truth is that no-one wants it now because of the problems associated with this type of EMD, and the fact that the domain may have picked up a penalty; something which isn't always removed when a domain changes hands either.

You can try a search for other EMDs from that contact lens list. If there is still a live EMD site for a phrase, then the chances are it was a better site, and more than likely de-optimized for that phrase. Either that or it's an abandoned site that the owner has left up for some other purpose.

Using the Way Back Machine to Check Domains

If your domain has never ranked properly, I'd recommend you check it at the Way Back Machine. You'll be able to see if your domain was used before you got your hands on it, and how. It is possible that the domain might have a penalty from before and that it carried over to you. If this is the case, you could file a reconsideration request at Google.

http://support.google.com/webmasters/bin/answer.py?hl=en&answer=35843

While it's not guaranteed to work, it might if Google can see that the domain has changed hands.

Keyword Stuffed Domains

Another potential problem with a domain name is keyword stuffing.

Let's suppose your website is selling cosmetic contact lenses. If your domain was **cosmetic-halloween-colored-contact-lenses.com,** then it's clearly stuffed with relevant keywords. This would get you into trouble, but even if it didn't, what would visitors think of a domain name like that? This type of domain is not one that I would be anxious to hold on to.

Back in March 2011, Google engineer Matt Cutts discussed the use of keywords in the domain name in a YouTube video:

http://www.youtube.com/watch?v=rAWFv43qubl

He suggested that a brandable domain is probably better than a keyword rich domain, and I agree. Despite being old, that video hints about the changes to come in the way keyword rich domains ranked at that time.

Of course, these are just general guidelines on domain names. Once you have your domain, there really isn't anything you can do about its name. Your choice is to either stick with it or move your site to a different domain. In this video, Matt Cutts offers some advice on moving a domain:

http://www.youtube.com/watch?v=wATxftE8ooE

Here are some other things to look out for which might indicate a low quality EMD site:

- Is the site specifically targeting that EMD phrase or does your site have a lot of quality content within the overall niche?
- Do you have a lot of backlinks with anchor text that matches the EMD phrase?
- Are there very few pages on your site?
- Reading your content, does there appear to be a bias towards using that EMD phrase as a way to try and help it rank better?

- Is that EMD phrase repeated numerous times on the homepage? What about other pages on the site?
- Is that phrase used in internal links pointing back to the homepage from other pages on the site?
- Is your on-site SEO specifically targeting that EMD phrase?

The Domain Name Checklist

- EMD? If yes, then be aware that this will work against you and you'll need to de-optimize the site for the phrase in the domain name.
- Is the EMD highly commercial in nature (not your brand)? If yes, then this might be a clear signal to Google that you are a spammer. The only option may be to move your site to a brand new domain.
- Is the domain name stuffed with keywords? If yes, there isn't much you can do with this other than to move the site to a better domain. Keyword stuffed domains look spammy and don't instil much confidence in visitors. Unless there is good reason to keep the domain, like it still makes good income or ranks well, then I'd seriously consider moving the site to a better, more brandable domain.
- Has your domain ever ranked properly? If not, then check its history at the Way Back Machine. Consider submitting a reconsideration request to Google if the site looks like a poor quality, spammy project from the past.

Checklist Point #2 - Web Page Real Estate

You should focus on two main areas when checking your web page real estate. These are "above the fold" and "sneaky links".

In January 2012, Google released a document that outlined a new "page layout algorithm improvement". You can read it here:

http://insidesearch.blogspot.com.es/2012/01/page-layout-algorithm-improvement.html

In releasing this change, Google were hoping to improve the user experience. No one likes to arrive at a website if all they see in their browser are Google ads, banners or email subscription forms. The general idea of this update was to penalise sites that didn't have much useful content above the fold. "Above the fold" simply means the viewable area in your browser before you scroll further down the page.

In the past, a lot of people made good money by throwing up quick, cheap "AdSense sites". These were designed to rank well in the SERPs, and many of them did just that. However, these sites showed visitors very little content, just money-generating adverts. On arrival, a visitor could click on an advert (and make the webmaster money), click the back button on their browser to return to the search page they came from, or they could scroll down the page to find the content. Because of the poor user experience on these sites, most people probably chose for one of the first two options as they figured the content would not be up to much. If something caught their eye in the adverts, they would click the ad as a way to get away from the page.

NOTE: If you are a member of Google AdSense yourself, you will have experienced the Google AdSense team advising you to put MORE adverts on your pages. The Google AdSense team seem to be at odds with what Google the Search Engine actually wants. Be aware that the two parts work separately and each has its own objectives and goals.

Look at your page above the fold. I'd actually recommend resizing your browser to 1024x768 (most people use this resolution or something higher these days, according to W3Schools.com):

http://www.w3schools.com/browsers/browsers_display.asp

Once you've set your browser resolution, see what shows above the fold on your site.

You then need to ask yourself if there is any meaningful content visible. If you removed the adverts from that area, what are you left with? Does it now offer value to visitors in terms of the remaining content above the fold? This is also an interesting test for your page as a whole. Is the remaining content of high quality if you remove the adverts from a page? The answer should be a resounding YES.

NOTE: If you have some adverts above the fold, you may be OK. On the page layout algorithm announcement, Google say this:

"This algorithmic change does not affect sites that place ads above-the-fold to a normal degree, but affects sites that go much further to load the top of the page with ads to an excessive degree, or that make it hard to find the actual original content on the page."

Sneaky Links in Footers, Headers or Elsewhere

Does your site have links in the footer? Links *per se* are not a problem, but if they are links with keyword rich anchor text, then they could be. If the links in your footer are there simply to make another webpage rank better for a keyword term, then there is a problem.

Look at your footer links, and if you see any that use keyword rich anchor text, remove them.

If you have other footer links to things like Twitter, Facebook, Contact, Privacy etc, then these are fine.

If the links are site-wide (appearing on every page on the site), you might like to add a "nofollow" attribute to those links.

Web Page Real Estate Checklist

- Resize your browser to 1024x768 and see what loads above the fold. Is the content useful? Are there too many adverts? If there are too many adverts, especially above the fold, consider removing (or moving) them.
- If you removed all of the adverts from the pages on your site, would those pages still offer the visitor what they are looking for?   If not, then the content is not good enough.
- Does your site have sneaky links in the footer, especially keyword rich anchor text links, either to other pages on your own site or to external sites? If yes, then get rid of them.

Checklist Point #3 - Site Structure

Is your site navigation helping your visitors find what they want quickly?

If you think in terms of needing every page on your site to be just one or two clicks away from the homepage at most, then you're on the right track.

Good website navigation should be intuitive to the visitor. They should immediately be able to see where they are at, and where they need to go for the information they require.

A good test here is to use a volunteer who has never been to your website before. Ask them to find a particular piece of information. Once they find it (if they find it), check to see how long it took them.

Include a Search Box

I'd highly recommend you have a search box on your website to help people find information quickly and effortlessly. If you are using WordPress, just know that the default search box that comes with the program is very poor. People won't be able to find what they want on a large site because WordPress doesn't rank its results by any kind of relevance, at least not any that I can detect.

An Example

On one of my websites, I had written an article on "vitamin A". I had also referenced vitamin A in 120+ other articles on the same site. The WordPress search box placed my main "vitamin A" article around position 125. That's not very good, and certainly not what I wanted to see.

WordPress or not, check out the search script your site is using. Do some searches. Does it return the most relevant pages in the results for search queries? If the results are not very good, then you need to look for a new search box script. There happens to be a very good one that I can recommend.

What if you could use Google's search engine to power the search box on your own site?

The good news is that you can. Google are kings of search and relevance, so using a search box powered by the search engine giant itself ensures people find the most relevant pages on your site quickly and easily. After installing the Google search box on my own site, I then searched again for "vitamin A". This time my main article came up as #1, just as it should do.

You can find out more about Google Custom Search here:

https://cse.google.com/cse/

If you have an AdSense account, you can create the search box within that account to use on your site. Note that this will display AdSense ads in the search results. Even so, you do make money if people click on any of those ads. If you want to opt-out of the adverts in your custom search engine, visit the link above as Google do have a paid option for this too.

Site-wide Links

Site-wide links are links that appear on all pages of your site. You do actually have to be careful and not overdo these. If you do have site-wide links, they should not use any keyword phrases that you are trying to rank for.

NOTE: Site-wide links can either be to pages on your own website or link out to different websites.

In the past, swapping site-wide links with webmasters of other websites was a common SEO practice, with the emphasis on "was". Today, I am saying don't do it. Google's quality guidelines clearly state that IF these links are there as an attempt to manipulate search rankings, they should not be used.

If you are a WordPress site owner, the typical site-wide links that come pre-installed with the program include the blogroll (a list of links that appears in your sidebar). I recommend you remove this from your site, even if you have edited the blogroll with more relevant websites.

Site-wide links are typically found in the header, footer or sidebars of a site. One of the most common forms of site-wide links is the main menu of the site. This menu links to the main areas of the website and serves a useful purpose. I would recommend that your main navigation menu is not keyword-focused. Instead, create this menu with the visitor in mind, as a useful way to help them find what they are looking for.

On smaller sites (10 or so pages), the main navigation menu usually links to all of the pages on the site. Again, avoid keyword-rich anchor text in these menus, and always think about what is most helpful to your visitors.

As your site grows, it becomes unnatural and impractical to link to all the pages from the main site-wide menu. A far better strategy is to create individual menus for each section of your site, and then put these menus on the pages in those sections. Let's consider "context-sensitive navigation".

Context-sensitive Navigation

The navigation system on your site can include menus in:

- The header
- The footer
- The sidebar
- Within the content area, usually at the end of a particular piece of content.

On larger websites, the navigation system you use should not be the same on every single page of the site. The navigation should change, depending on the page and its location on the site. I'm not suggesting every page on your website has a different navigation menu, but certainly sections of your site could use their own custom menus.

The easiest way to think about this is with an example. Let's say you have a health site and the visitor is on a page about osteoporosis. A menu that could help the visitor would contain links to other articles about osteoporosis or conditions that cause the disease. You could still include a navigation "block" linking to the main areas within the site, but you'd also include more specific options for your visitor, related to the current article they are reading.

Let's consider another example. If you had a travel site and a visitor was on a page talking about restaurants in Bali, it would make perfect sense to have navigation options that show other articles on Bali, maybe hotels, attractions, and surfing, etc.

For a third and final example, let's say you have an ecommerce website that sells baby products. You might have a main site-wide menu that includes links to all of the main sections/categories on your site. This might include things such as strollers, cots, car seats and so on. Now, if your visitor is browsing the section on strollers, a menu with links to 2-seat strollers, jogging strollers, double and triple strollers, etc., would be very helpful. Always think in terms of how your navigation can best serve your visitors as that will help to keep you focussed when putting your site together.

This type of dynamic navigation is clearly easier and more practical to implement on larger sites. However, if you have a small site with a site-wide menu, do look at your navigation and make sure your links are not keyword-focused, and that the navigation actually helps, and not hinders the visitor experience.

A Tip for WordPress Users

Three plugins I recommend for helping you create a dynamic navigation system are:

Dynamic Widgets: http://wordpress.org/extend/plugins/dynamic-widgets/. This allows you to set up different sidebar menus (created as widgets) in different areas of your site.

Yet Another Related Posts Plugin (YARPP):
http://wordpress.org/extend/plugins/yet-another-related-posts-plugin/. This allows you to set up a related posts section after each piece of content. When a visitor gets to the end of an article, they'll see a list of related posts and be tempted to click through to one. This type of internal linking is also beneficial from a search engine perspective as it links related content together.

C.I. Backlinks: http://ezseonews.com/cibacklinks
This is the plugin I personally use. It allows me to "automatically" link internal pages on my site. It works the way I do, because I helped design it and consulted at every step of its development.

Content Organization on Your Server (Non-WordPress Sites)

Organization of your content on the server and your site's navigation system go hand-in-hand. One mirrors the other. Well organized content is stored in a logical, intuitive manner, which should reflect in the navigation system.

The physical organization on your server is only important if you are building your website using something like HTML, which stores webpages as separate files. This doesn't apply to WordPress because it does not save content as individual files.

Let's use a theoretical example of a pet website. It might have content written about:

- Fish
- Birds
- Dogs
- Reptiles
- Amphibians
- Cats

There should be a folder/directory on your server for each of these content areas, and all files need saving into their corresponding folders. You see how this physical organization would mirror the navigation system of your site.

The first thing for you to check is whether your content is properly organized. In other words, are the right files placed in the right folders on your server, that is, are all dog related articles physically located inside the dog folder (aka a directory), cats in the cat folder, and so on?

If the dog section on the site grows, we'll need to add to the structure of the folders/directories on our server. When the site gets bigger it's time to re-organize our content, in the exact same way we did with the navigation system earlier.

For example, if your pet project was an informational site, you could add the following sub-folders under your "dog" folder on the server:

- Training
- Toys
- Beds
- Food & treats

Each of these sub-folders would then store the content related to those files. So for example, all articles on dog training would be located in the "/dogs/training/" sub folder on your server.

If your site sold pets, perhaps a more logical way to organize the content would be to have sub-folders like:

- Alsatians
- Terriers
- Dalmatians
- Huskies

...And so on.

By efficiently organizing your content into logical folders on your server, the URLs of these pages would now look something like this:

mypetsite.com/dogs/training/clickers.html

mypetsite.com/dogs/training/choke-chain.html
mypetsite.com/dogs/training/walking-to-heel.html
mypetsite.com/dogs/food/mixers.html
mypetsite.com/dogs/food/tinned-dog-food.html
mypetsite.com/dogs/food/snacks.html

These URLs give the search engines big clues about the content. For example, the search engines would know that all six of those web pages were about dogs. They would also know that three of them relate to training dogs, while three others relate to dog food.

This type of physical organization helps the search engines categorize and rank your content. This is because your pages end up in "silos" of related material, with links between related content, thus joining them all together.

This folder organization on your server should match the menu navigation on your site.

NOTE: If you are using WordPress, you can get the same types of URLs by using categories. While categories are not physical locations like directories/folders on the server, they still serve the same purpose in categorizing your content into logical groups.

WordPress actually takes things a stage further and includes a feature called tags. You can think of tags as an additional way to classify your content, the main way being with categories. I won't go into how to use WordPress categories and tags in this book, other than to give you a couple of quick tips:

1. Never use a word or phrase as both a category and a tag. If it's a really important part of your site structure, it's a category. If it's less important, use a tag.

2. Never use a tag for just one post. If a tag is important, it will be used on several posts on your site. If it's not, then it's not important, so delete it.

Internal Linking of Content

When one of your pieces of content references information that is elsewhere on the site, it makes perfect sense to link to that other page within the body of your content. If we look at this Wikipedia page you can see a lot of links:

Glutathione

From Wikipedia, the free encyclopedia

Glutathione (GSH) is an important antioxidant in plants, animals, fungi, and some bacteria and archaea, preventing damage to important cellular components caused by reactive oxygen species such as free radicals, peroxides, lipid peroxides and heavy metals.[2] It is a tripeptide with a gamma peptide linkage between the carboxyl group of the glutamate side-chain and the amine group of cysteine (which is attached by normal peptide linkage to a glycine).

Thiol groups are reducing agents, existing at a concentration around 5 mM in animal cells. Glutathione reduces disulfide bonds formed within cytoplasmic proteins to cysteines by serving as an electron donor. In the process, glutathione is converted to its oxidized form, glutathione disulfide (GSSG), also called L-(−)-glutathione.

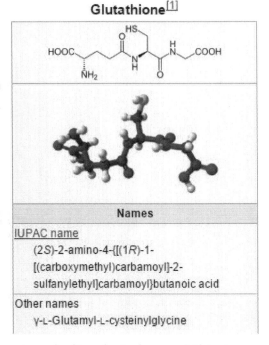

Glutathione[1]

Names
IUPAC name
(2S)-2-amino-4-{[(1R)-1-[(carboxymethyl)carbamoyl]-2-sulfanylethyl]carbamoyl}butanoic acid
Other names
γ-L-Glutamyl-L-cysteinylglycine

NOTE: The actual links on Wikipedia pages are not underlined. I changed this to make the links easier to see in this book.

Each of these links goes to another web page on the Wikipedia website. Not only does this internal linking help the search engine spiders (programs that visit websites and read their pages and other information) to index the pages on the site, but it also helps the visitor to navigate more easily. If someone reading this article wants to learn more about something mentioned in the piece, they can easily click the relevant link and read about it in more detail before returning to the original page to continue reading.

Internal linking helps both visitors and search engines. Links with anchor text tell the search engine what the page is about. The only recommendation I'd make with internal linking is that you vary the anchor text in those links, much like you do with external links pointing into your website.

I did an experiment on internal linking and published the results on my site:

http://ezseonews.com/backlinks/internal-linking-seo/

The article gives you tips on using internal linking to best effect, and the results of an experiment I ran.

Essentially, I took one of my webpages that ranked at #190 for a particular phrase I was targeting. Using nothing but internal links, I managed to move that page up to position #14 in the Google SERPs. That indicates to me that Google like internal linking when it helps the visitor and it clearly helps pages rank better too.

The things I'd recommend you look at on your own site are as follows:

1. Do you make use of internal linking in the body of the content, much like Wikipedia?

2. Do you vary internal link anchor texts that point to a specific page?

3. For any particular anchor text, make sure you only ever link to one URL with it. Using the same anchor text to point to two or more different URLs is confusing, especially for the search engines.

Site Structure Checklist

- Is your navigation intuitive?
- Are all of the pages on your site just one or two clicks away from the homepage? They should be.
- Do you have site-wide links in the sidebar?
- Do you have site-wide links in the header?
- Do you have site-wide links in the footer?

NOTE: Site-wide links with keyword-rich anchor text are potentially the most damaging.

- If you have a large site, do you use dynamic menus, which change depending on the section of the site the visitor is viewing?
- Do you have a search box? If it is a WordPress default search box, I highly recommend you switch to a more efficient script like Google's custom search.
- Do you internally link the pages of your website from within the body of your content, and not just via the navigation menus or a related posts menu?
- Is your content logically organized into "silos" where all related content is in the same category or folder? If necessary (e.g. on a large site), do you use sub-folders to help make the navigation even more intuitive?
- If you are using WordPress, do you have any tags that are only used once or twice? If so, remove them.
- If you are using WordPress, do you have any tags that are identical to some of your category names? If so, remove them. Never use a phrase for a tag if it is being used (or will be used) as a category.

Checklist Point #4 - Comments

Visitor Contact

A visitor-friendly site is one which offers your visitors the chance to interact with you.

Something ALL websites should have is a contact form.

Something else that I highly recommend you include is a comment form so that visitors can remark on your content. This might not be applicable in all cases, but in general, visitors do like to know there is a real person behind a site, and often like to have their say on content that has appealed to them. Not only does a comment form build trust, but it also builds social proof as new visitors get to see that others before them have also left comments on the pages.

There are contact form scripts and comment form scripts available for HTML websites. Content management systems, like WordPress, have the comments built in, and contact forms are readily available as plugins.

I recommend you implement both on your site if it makes sense to do so.

If you already have a comment form on your site, check the comment settings. If you have your comments set to "auto-approve", then set it to "administrator approval" so that ALL comments have to go by you first. If you set up comments for auto-approval, you will more than likely get a lot of spam comments published, and they could bring the quality of your site down. Get too many of these spam comments on your pages, and they might cost you a penalty, especially if they link out to "bad neighbourhoods".

Bad neighbourhoods? OK, for anyone not familiar with the terminology, let me explain what a "bad neighbourhood" is.

Most spammers leave comments with the sole intention of getting a backlink and potential new traffic to their own web site. Many of these will be low quality sites, porn sites, gambling, or other types of sites that you would not want to associate with your project. Google refers to these types of sites as "bad neighbourhoods". In addition, there is nothing to stop someone who has left a comment on your site (and had it approved some time ago), from redirecting their link to a bad neighbourhood at a later date. To be safe, make all comments on your site **nofollow**.

Once everything is set up properly, go through **every single comment** on your site and delete any that are either fake or blatant spam.

Fake Comments

Fake comments are those that you - pretending to be someone else - wrote so that your page appears visited and popular. Fake comments are those that someone you asked (or likely hired) wrote for you (there are many freelancers out there offering such services). A lot of webmasters add fake comments to their site to make it look a little more active than it actually is. It was a good idea once, like so many other things in the past, but today I advise you not to do it. Most of the time, fake comments are easy to spot and don't exactly instil trust once you've been rumbled.

Typical ways that fake comments stand out are:

1. Several comments posted within a very short space of time of each another, and then nothing; at least for good a while afterwards.

2. Groups of fake comments rarely have author images (Gravatars) associated with the comment, which makes them stand out even more.

3. Comments are "bland" and don't really add anything to the content/conversation.

4. Comments are copied and pasted from another website like Amazon.

Spam Comments

Spam comments are not always easy to spot. They are written with the sole intention of getting a valuable backlink, so spammers have become creative in the way they do their spamming. There are even software tools available that help spammers to carry out mass-scale spamming of comment-enabled websites.

As a rule, don't approve any comment that is "stroking your ego", or "patting you on the back for a job well done".

One way spammers try to get their comments approved is to say things like "Great article" or "This is amazing, I've told my friends about this". Here is one I got recently:

> Submitted on 2013/03/05 at 08:42
>
> You blog post is just completely quality and informative. Many new facts and information which I have not heard about before. Keep sharing more blog posts.

While I have no doubt that this comment is true ;), sadly it is also blatant spam.

This flattery is supposed to stroke the ego of the webmaster so that it gets through the approval process. Don't approve these types of comments UNLESS you know the comment is legitimate, i.e. you recognize the commenter. Note too that comments like these make absolutely no reference to the article. In other words, they could just as easily be on a page about how to make cupcakes as one which looks deeply into astrophysics.

However, other comment spam is not always so obvious and disguised much better than the example above.

For example, a spammer might find a page they want a backlink from on the "health benefits of zinc". They'll then go and find an article on the web about this topic and grab a quote from it to use as their own comment. The quote will look like a real comment about your article, but will in fact be content copied from another website.

This type of comment spam is often difficult to catch, except to say that in most cases it won't look quite right in the context of your article, not least because it will probably be overly formal and make no "specific" reference to your post or any of the other commenter's remarks. If in doubt, grab the content of the comments, put it in quotes, and then search Google for it.

Another type of comment spam is where the commenter is just trying to drive your traffic to their website. Here is an example of that:

> Submitted on 2013/03/08 at 13:34
>
> I would certainly not recommend 1&1. My recent experiences are detailed on my blog, here;
>
> I have always found Bluehost easy to use, Hostgator I find a little "clunky" but my favourite has to be Dreamhost. They had a few issues in the past but everything works like a dream for me and I find their unique control panel interface so easy to use.

You can see that I've blurred out the URL linking to his web page.

His page is a basic review of his favourite web hosting company (which does include his experiences with 1&1), and an affiliate link to that host. He left a comment that I would have otherwise approved, but not with that link to his web page. He is probably targeting any "high traffic" website that has reviewed the 1&1 web host, or even Hostgator, and leaving similar reviews in the hope that he can piggy-back off their traffic as well as benefit from the relevant backlink.

General Rule for Approving Comments

Only approve comments if:

1. It is clear from the comment that the person has read the article.
2. The comment adds to the article, like another point of view on something specific to the post.
3. If you know that the person is real because you recognize their name (but only if the comment is also not spammy).

Obviously these are just guidelines. In the field of battle, you'll have to make some tough decisions, but I recommend only keeping the best comments that you're sure are genuine. Delete EVERYTHING else. As you become familiar with comment spam, in all its forms, you will intuitively know what is genuine and what is not.

Comments Checklist

- Does your website have a comments section where visitors can leave comments, thoughts and questions?

- Does your website have a Contact Us form?
- If you have comments enabled, are you manually approving all comments? You should be.
- Check through all of the comments on your site and remove any fake or spam comments. In fact, remove any comment where the sole purpose is to get a backlink to a website.
- Make comment links nofollow by default.
- Going forward, only approve legitimate comments where it is clear the visitor has read your content and added to the conversation with their insight.

Checklist Point #5 - Social Presence

Under the umbrella of social presence, I include two things:

1. The website and its author have a social presence on social media sites.
2. The website has social sharing "buttons" on its pages to allow visitors to easily share the content to their own social media followers.

Check your website. Do you have both of these things present?

Let's look to see exactly what I mean here, as well as give you some ideas for a "bare minimum" social approach.

The Website and Website Author Has a Social Presence

The three main social channels I'd recommend you look at are:

1. Facebook

2. Twitter

3. Google Plus

I recommend you consider these in that order of priority as well. If you have a Facebook account you can easily setup a Facebook Page for your website. You can then link to the Facebook page from a prominent position on your pages.

You can see how I have this set up on one of my sites. Visitors can follow me on Twitter, Facebook or add me to a circle on Google plus.

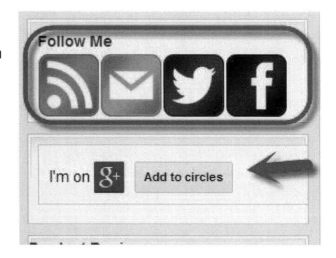

Your Facebook page offers your visitors an additional channel for starting a "conversation" with you and your audience. From your point of view, you can post updates to that page which include things like:

- Tips and tricks for your industry/niche.
- Current news in your niche.
- Interesting articles you find around the web.
- New posts on your site (this can be automated).
- Videos, images, etc.
- Current special offers from your website.
- Anything else that is relevant to your site and niche.

Think of your Facebook page as an extension of your website. A Facebook page that has a thriving community can rank well in Google, plus give your "brand" a huge amount of social proof. It's so easy to setup that I recommend all websites have a Facebook page.

As far as Twitter is concerned, it's also very easy to setup an account for your website. You can even setup your website to send a tweet to your Twitter account automatically, every time you publish new content on your site. You can of course send tweets with information related to your niche too (the same kind of stuff that you can post on Facebook). Services like Hootsuite: http://hootsuite.com allows you to schedule tweets (as well as Facebook and Google Plus posts) in advance, which can prove useful.

As your Twitter following increases, you'll automatically be increasing your "authority" in the eyes of your visitors. Let's face it, if you have a Twitter account with 10,000+ followers, a lot of people will think: "Wow, this site must be good if it has that many followers. I must follow too".

Now, before you think you've already tried Twitter and only ever managed to get a handful of followers, let me tell you that there are ways to increase the number. I wrote an article called "How to get more Twitter Followers" where I show you some methods for increasing Twitter followers.

http://ezseonews.com/review/how-to-get-more-twitter-followers/

While it's true that your Twitter list may not be too responsive when built the way I suggest in my article, that's not really the point. The main point of this to begin with is to boost the social proof on your site. As your site grows in authority, you will find your Twitter following increases naturally, with more targeted individuals. It then becomes more than just a social proof thing. It becomes a useful tool for business.

When you have a Twitter account, make sure you link to it from your website so that people can follow you (as I did in the previous screenshot). Once the Twitter following has grown to the point where you are proud of it, you may want to head on over to: http://twittercounter.com and get a "badge" for your website. The badge displays how many Twitter followers you currently have. This all helps to add authority to your site, and the more authority your site gets from visitors, the more authority it gets from the search engines that monitor visitor behaviour.

The final social media platform that I recommend getting involved with is Google Plus. You can setup a Google Plus "Page" for your website and post to it, in much the same way you do to Facebook. Google plus works in a very different way though, and it's beyond the scope of this book to teach you all the ins and outs of Google Plus.

OK, so those are the three main social media channels I suggest you get involved with.

Let's now look at how you can give your visitors the opportunity to share your content with their own followers, using social sharing buttons.

Social Media Share "Buttons"

If I show you an example, I am sure you'll recognize what I am talking about:

Typically, social media sharing buttons appear in a "panel", either above, below (or above AND below) the content on the page. This panel can be horizontal or even floating vertically (as in the screenshot above) over the webpage on the right or left, or in a sidebar.

In my screenshot, the top social button is Facebook, the second Twitter and the third Google Plus. Again, I'd recommend concentrating on these three above all others.

NOTE: The bottom one in the screenshot is another service called Buffer, which isn't currently on my essential list. It could be in the future though, so you may want to read up on that service here:

http://bufferapp.com/

Other social media sites you might like to have buttons for include Pinterest (if your site has a lot of images that you want shared) and StumbleUpon (a discovery engine that finds and recommends web content to its 25 million+ users).

For WordPress users, there are a stack of plugins to add this sharing functionality to your site.

For HTML sites, you'll need to find a script that has these features, or manually go to each social media site and grab the button code to include in your own social media "panel".

What Do These Buttons Do Exactly?

These buttons give visitors to your site the opportunity to share your webpage with their own social media followers.

For example, if I clicked on the Tweet button in the panel above, a short Tweet is constructed automatically, with the URL and title of that page included in the tweet.

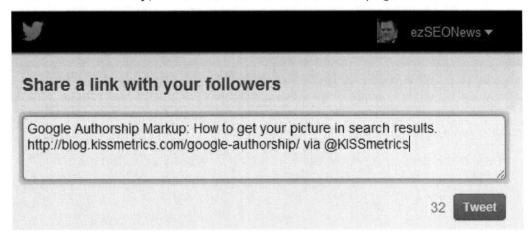

You can see at the end of the Tweet how Twitter has added "via @KISSmetrics". This sends "KISSmetrics" (the author of the content) an auto-notification that someone has re-tweeted their content. This is one way how you can connect with the leaders in your niche.

When you have these social share buttons on your website, your visitors become your army of promoters, as long as your content is good enough, of course.

So, check your site. Do you have social sharing buttons? If not, I highly recommend that you add them (at least for the main three, namely Facebook, Twitter, and Google+).

NOTE: Google do index tweets and probably use them as a social signal in ranking (although probably only for a limited time). Google also knows how many Facebook likes your content gets and may use that as a social signal too. And of course, Google obviously monitor Google pluses.

Social Presence Checklist

- Does your website have a presence on Facebook?
- Does your website have a presence on Twitter?
- Does your website have a presence on Google plus?
- Does your website have social sharing buttons that allow your visitors to share your content with their own social media followers? Remember, you should include Twitter, Facebook and Google plus as a bare minimum.

Checklist Point #6 - Would You Trust the Site?

This section looks at the trust levels for your site. We've already discussed some of the things that can help people trust you and your site, but let's now look at a more comprehensive list.

People like to deal with real people. So when they arrive at your site, do they know who they are dealing with?

The All-important Photo

A lot of split testing has shown that a photo of a real person increases conversions. From my own experience, the photos that work the best are NOT the ones that look like "stock photos", but those which look like a real person, or the person next door, so to speak. There's a reason for this. Websites that show real people help to build trust. When someone trusts your site they are more likely to follow through with your calls-to-action (CTA).

So where are the best places to put a photo on your site? Well, it really depends on the type of site you have, but a photo in the header or the sidebar usually works well. Here is one found in a sidebar:

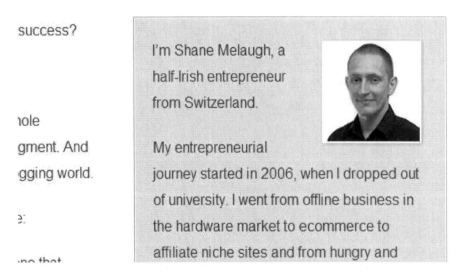

See how Shane looks like a "real person" in that natural style of photo.

The style of Shane's photo is very different from many of the photo's you'd get from a stock photo site:

More items by ollyi

Whichever photo you use, make sure you look like a real person and not a photographic model. You want people to trust the image and anything that looks too glitzy may not appear genuine in the eyes of your visitors.

My favourite place to include a photo is in an author's resource box, at the end of each piece of content. Here is an example:

There's a separate case in progress that may lead to the Microsoft patent being ruled invalid, but that doesn't appear to have any bearing on this case at the moment.

A final decision is expected in May.

Related Entries
- Google In Privacy Flap With Germans Over New iOS Maps
- Google, Microsoft Cooperate To Invalidate Broad Online Mapping Patent

Related Topics: Google: Legal | Google: Maps & Local | Google: Outside US | Legal: Patents | Top News

 About The Author: Matt McGee is Editor-In-Chief of Search Engine Land. His news career includes time spent in TV, radio, and print journalism. His web career continues to include a small number of SEO and social media consulting clients, as well as regular speaking engagements at marketing events around the U.S. He blogs at Small Business Search Marketing and can be found on Twitter at @MattMcGee and/or on Google Plus. You can read Matt's disclosures on his personal blog. See more articles by Matt McGee

Connect with the author via: Email | Twitter | Google+ | LinkedIn ◄───

This author's bio box is at the end of the article. Notice how Matt includes links to his social channels underneath the bio.

If you don't have a photograph of the author or owner on your site, I recommend you add one ASAP.

The "About Us" Page

Every website should have an About Us page. Those that do, often find it's one of the most visited pages on the site. The About Us page is something that many webmasters skip over, but it really does help to build trust when people can find out more about you and your site. It also gives your visitors an opportunity to learn more about you on a human level. They like to find out what drives you and your site. This can be very important on dry, technical types of sites. If you want more advice on how to create a great "About Us" page, I recommend you read this article:

http://socialmediatoday.com/bryan-eisenberg/1006526/about-us-page-social-world

Bryan Eisenberg offers some brilliant advice. He gets you started by answering some very simple questions.

Comments Enabled

We've already talked about comments earlier in this book. Make sure you have a comment system installed on your site so that visitors can leave feedback. Good feedback can only help build trust and social proof for you and your brand.

Does the Site Pretend to Be a Merchant?

This specifically refers to affiliate sites who send traffic to a merchant site in return for making commissions on any sale.

Some affiliate marketers don't make it clear that they are just an intermediary in the sales process. They let visitors believe they are the actual merchant.

A typical case of this is when marketers use links that say, "Buy here" or "Buy now", without letting customers know they'll be visiting a different site to complete the transaction. Look at it from a visitor point of view. Don't you think it's a bit of a shock to be on one site, click the "buy" button, and then end up on say Amazon, for example? Sure it is.

Is the Site/Webmaster a Recognized Authority?

Being an authority means you are recognized as someone to trust within your niche. It's something you can achieve relatively easily if you do one thing:

BE EVERYWHERE!

Part of the reason I look for a social presence from the websites I critique is because these help to build authority. If someone finds your Facebook page (where they see your photo) in Google, and likes it, then when they go to your website (and see your photo) and think, "Hmmm, I've seen this person before and they know what they're talking about." The same goes for any social media channel. The important thing here is to only ever share quality information to those channels, and never, whatever you do, get into heated debates with anyone who happens to disagree with you.

One method I use to extend my reach into a niche is to use the same photograph (either me, or my persona for a project), on my website, my Facebook page, Twitter & Google+ pages, and as a Gravatar: http://en.gravatar.com/, which is set up on the main email address for the site. A Gravatar is just an image associated with an email address. Whenever you post on forums, or comment on Gravatar-enabled blogs, your photo shows next to your post. People will start to recognize you everywhere they go within that niche, because you are "Everywhere". If the information you share through these channels is good, then you can quickly build a reputation as someone to trust, and become a real authority figure within your niche.

NOTE: Being a recognized authority is particularly important on medical sites. You need to know what you are talking about first and foremost, but secondly, people need to trust you. If you are a doctor, or have specific training related to your site, let your visitors know this.

If your site relates to health or medicine, are you a recognized authority? If not, then that is something you might like to work on.

It's still possible to write good content as an independent researcher on health related issues, even if you don't have any particular educational or occupational qualifications. However, to become trusted you must quote all your reliable reference sources, and not just write things casually like, "Report's suggest", or "A study done some years ago found that...", etc.

Other Reasons People Don't Trust Your Website?

There are a few other reasons why people won't trust a website. I won't go into details on each of these reasons; I'll just list them. If any of these things are missing from your own website, then you might want to consider making some adjustments (recommended).

The Distrust Checklist

- No Contact page.
- No privacy page.
- No business address or phone number, or nothing that is clearly displayed.
- Site doesn't seem to have been updated in years.
- No testimonials.
- Copyright notice on the website is out of date.
- Lack of "trust symbols", e.g. Better Business Bureau, VeriSign, McAfee, etc.
- Web pages with typos, spelling mistakes or grammatical errors.
- Lack of response from YOU where visitors have posted comments/questions.
- Bad reviews.
- Poorly targeted emails, and difficulty unsubscribing from your newsletter.

The Trust Checklist

- Does the site have a photo of the webmaster/author of the content?
- Does your site have an About Us page?
- Are comments enabled?
- Does your site pretend to be a merchant?

- Is the author of your site a recognized authority in the niche/industry?
- Are you using a Gravatar set up on the email address that you use for your site?
- Does your site display your business address, preferably with a phone number?
- When was your site last updated?
- If appropriate, are there any testimonials and if yes, are they up to date?
- Does the copyright notice on your website display the correct year?
- Do you display any trust symbols (if appropriate)?
- Check all content for spellings and grammatical errors. Check your navigation systems for these errors as well.
- Are there any unanswered comments on your site?

Checklist Point #7 – Bounce Rates & Time on Site

Google most certainly monitor two metrics as a way of determining visitor satisfaction levels. The first is the bounce rate and the second is the time they spend on your site.

According to Google:

> *"Bounce rate is the percentage of visits that go only one page before exiting a site."*

In other words, someone only views one page on your site before exiting. Typically, high bounce rates are bad for your site's reputation. It usually means people are not finding what they want on your site and therefore feel the need to leave and look elsewhere.

Time spent on site is the length of time a visitor stays on your site overall. A low time on site may indicate a problem with your content, since people aren't sticking around to read it.

If you haven't set up Google Analytics on your website, I recommend you do so. Once it's set up, leave your site to collect new data for a month or so before trying to analyse these metrics. Then, go through your analytics to find pages that have high bounce rates AND low time spent on the page(s).

A page with a high bounce rate but with high time on the page is not a problem. Look at these examples:

Avg. Time on Page	Entrances	Bounce Rate ↓
00:52:18	3	66.67%
00:00:00	2	50.00%
00:17:41	2	50.00%
00:00:00	4	50.00%

The top page in the list has a bounce rate of 66.67% (the site average is around 10% so 66.67% is high). Despite the high bounce rate, I am happy with this page because there were three visitors, with an average time on that page of 52 minutes, 18 seconds. This tells me that the visitor must have found the information useful and engaging, even though they didn't visit any other pages on the site.

Similarly, the second page I highlighted above has a bounce rate of 50%, this time with two visits. However, the average time on that page was 17 minutes 41 seconds, so again, those two visitors must have found what they were looking for (or at least found it interesting) before they hit their back button and returned to Google.

The two pages that would concern me are the examples that I haven't circled. Both pages had an average time on site of 0 minutes. I would go and look at these pages in more depth, and over a longer period, to see whether there may have been a glitch in the reporting during the above screenshot, or, whether these pages historically have high bounce rates and a low time spent on the page.

What you need to do is identify pages with high bounce rates AND low time spent on the page. Once you find them, you need to work out why visitors are not satisfied with what they see. If the content is good, maybe it's just not a good match for the search phrase they found you with on Google. Or maybe something else is pushing them away from the page(s). You need to look for ways to increase the visitor time on these pages (and hopefully decrease the bounce rates).

Bounce Rate & Time on Site Checklist

Install Google Analytics and allow it to run for a few weeks so that you have sufficient data to work with. Once you're ready, check your bounce rate and time spent on site.

- Are your average bounce rates high?
- Are visitors spending a long or short time on your site?
- Look for specific pages where bounce rate is high AND time on site is low. Try to work out why these pages are suffering and fix them accordingly. Perhaps your page title does not accurately match the page content? This would mean that your listing in Google is misleading people to click through to your page, so when they do arrive there, they are disappointed and click the back button. Always consider tweaking page title and Meta description tags on any page with a high bounce rate, and then monitor the situation to see if your changes improve things.

Checklist Point #8 – Legal Pages

There are certain pages on a website that I call "legal" pages. These are things like:

- Privacy Policy
- Disclaimers (including any medical or earnings disclaimers).
- Contact Us
- Terms
- About Us (we talked about this earlier in terms of visitor trust).
- Any other documents that should be displayed on your site. These might include things like cookie policy, anti-spam policy, outbound link disclaimer, and so on.

Does your website include all of the necessary documents?

This article will help you decide which legal documents you need:

http://www.seqlegal.com/blog/what-legal-documents-do-i-need-my-new-website

They also offer webmasters free "legal" documents here:

http://www.seqlegal.com/free-legal-documents

There are "credits" written into these free documents that need to be left in place, but for a small fee (currently £3.50), you can get that credit removed.

Legal Pages Checklist

Not all of these pages are necessary for all types of website, so check which pages your site needs and add them if they are missing.

- Do you have a privacy page?
- Do you have a disclaimer page?
- Do you have a "terms of use" and conditions page (TOS)?
- Do you have a contact page?
- Do you have an about us page?
- Do you have a medical disclaimer page?
- Do you have an email policy page?
- Do you have an outbound link policy page?

Checklist Point #9 - Content Quality

This is a huge component of modern SEO.

If Content Is Bad, Getting Everything Else Right Won't Fix the Site

You need to have a website that you are proud of. More than that, you need to have a website that you would be proud to show anyone at Google. Content is what separates an average site from a great one, and the best way to understand what Google is looking for is to ask yourself one simple question:

"Could the content appear in a magazine?"

I actually took this question from the Google blog, in a piece about quality content. This is what you should be aiming for; this is what Google want.

Obviously ecommerce sites have a lot of pages that wouldn't satisfy this question, but it's certainly a great question to ask on any article-based content.

Here is another question that can apply to most types of content:

"Is your content the type of content that people will want to bookmark, or share socially?"

NOTE: Google can certainly detect bookmarks and social shares, so they are able to use them as indicators if they choose to. However, forget Google for a moment. Having content that people want to bookmark is a good indication that it is of value to visitors. This means they will want to share and link to your pages naturally, without being coerced or tricked. Remember how we talked about "link bait" in the first half of this book? Well, you should always be thinking "link bait" whenever you create new content.

Who Is a Good Judge of Your Content?

The biggest problem I have found concerning content quality is that webmasters themselves are not very impartial when it comes to judging their own material. If you can, it's always better to get someone else to honestly evaluate your content for you.

Besides the quality of your writing, there are a number of other things to look out for as you assess the content on your website. Here is a checklist (in no particular order):

- Have other websites copied and published the content?

  This is a common problem, though these scraper sites are usually very low quality and recognized for what they are by Google. In the past, these types of sites could hurt your rankings, but as Google developed its algorithms, this method of copying other people's content has become less of an issue.

To check whether your content has been stolen you could use a site like Copyscape: http://www.copyscape.com. Alternatively, grab a sentence or two from your web page and search for it on Google between quotes. If that block of text is on any other website(s), Google search will let you know. Here is an example of what it looks like when you do this type of search and other sites have copied (stolen) your content:

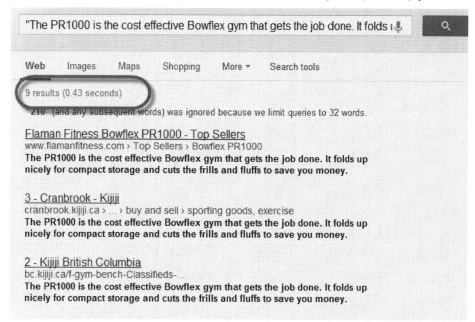

See how there are nine results in Google, each with the identical text.

If other sites have stolen your content and used it on their own sites, I'd recommend you contact those other sites and ask them to take the content down right away, informing them that they're breaching your copyright. Usually the threat of getting their hosting company involved is enough for most people to remove your stuff. Here is an article written by Jim Edwards that addresses the problem of copyright infringement:

http://ezseonews.com/general/internet-copyright-infringement-and-how-to-handle-it/

The article is a little old, but it still has great advice.

If you prefer, you can hire services to deal with content thieves. DMCA: http://www.dmca.com is one; although I've never used them, so cannot personally vouch for their service.

OK, let's now look at some other "quality" guidelines to consider:

- Product reviews unbiased?
  If you have product reviews on your site, are they unbiased, or positive, positive and more hyped up positives? See, the thing is you need to share both sides of the story. Consumers know that ALL products have some things that are not perfect, so you need to highlight all sides.

- More than just a rehash of the merchant site content?

  On the topic of reviews, is the content just a rehash of what you can find on the merchant site or perhaps Amazon? Your reviews need to be PERSONAL. Readers must know that you have personally tried the product and therefore your review must contain insights not seen on ANY other website. Write your review from personal, first-hand experience.

- Affiliate link disclaimer?
  If your site is an affiliate site, do you have an affiliate link disclaimer? Do people on your site know that you are not the actual merchant?

This all comes back to the issue of trust. I realize that an affiliate link disclaimer can hurt conversion rates, so try to tell your visitors in such a way that they don't mind you being an affiliate. After all, you are helping them with their buying decision, aren't you?

In my experience, if someone reads an impartial review by someone who has actually used the product, then they don't mind clicking a link knowing it's an affiliate link. If they read a hyped up sales pitch, on the other hand, and then find out your link is an affiliate link, then you're going to lose both trust and respect.

- Keyword stuffing

  Keyword stuffing is really bad SEO. In the past, webmasters knew that adding keywords to their content would make it rank better for those keywords. Consequently, articles often became stuffed with keyword phrases. Today, that kind of thing will get your site penalized or even booted out of Google SERPs altogether.

As you read your content, ask yourself if it looks like it's written for a human or a search engine. If the latter, then re-write it or scrap it altogether.

A quick test for keyword stuffing is to read your content carefully (or get a friend to read it). Can you pick out phrases you think the article was designed to rank for by the way it repeats a phrase? Or maybe it's written with slight grammatical errors just that so a particular phrase could be inserted?

You MUST take out any keyword stuffed content. Whether that means re-writing it or deleting it, that's your choice.

My advice when you are writing content is to WRITE NATURALLY!

If you hear anyone talking about keyword densities, ignore them. The correct density for any word or phrase on a page is the density that it ends up with when written naturally. It might be 2%, it might be 1%, and it might even be 0.1% or 0%. Bear that in mind. As you read your content, try to see if any word or phrase seems overused more than is natural.

- Fluff rating

  Fluff rating is a term I use with my students.

  Looking at the free dictionary: http://www.thefreedictionary.com/fluff, the definition of fluff is:

Something of little substance or consequence, especially:

*a. **Light or superficial entertainment**: The movie was just another bit of fluff from Hollywood.*

*b. **Inflated or padded material**: The report was mostly fluff, with little new information.*

Part (b) is exactly what I am referring to - an article that goes on and on but doesn't really say anything.

Webmasters have typically tried to increase the length of their content because they think that more words rank better. This means that an article that could be covered in just 400 words in a quality piece, is now stretched out to say 600 words - 200 of which are fluff - and only included to raise the word count. What effectively happens in cases like this is that an otherwise good article is watered down and becomes less valuable and/or readable.

An article that says very little, despite its word count, has a high fluff rating and should be deleted or re-written to provide quality information on a given topic.

- Information duplicated on multiple articles

  Does information on one page of your site appear on other pages as well? In other words, is there a big overlap between the content on the various pages of your site? If so, you need to remove it. If two or more articles are so closely related that they share the same information, consider merging those pieces into one big article.

  The pages on a website should all contain different information and there should be a bare minimum of content overlap.

- Check the sitemap

  A sitemap is a great way to check your content. As you look through the sitemap, are there instances where two pages have very similar filenames, or titles? If so, are those two pages covering the same information? If yes, then you might want to combine them into a single quality article.

A common strategy for building a website is to carry out keyword research, and then write content around the keyword(s) that have high demand and low competition. One problem with this approach is that two or more phrases - which basically mean the same thing - can become the basis for separate articles.

A site might have separate articles based on each of these phrases:

- Best vacuum
- Best vacuum cleaner
- Which is the best vacuum?

Can you see how those three phrases are saying the same thing? So how can there be three separate articles for these phrases?

Here is an example that I found on one website:

http://v████████████████ ███/room-addition/

http://█████████████████ ███/room-additions/

This website has an article on "room addition" and another on "room additions".

Here is another example:

~~The mood of the party is set right at the beginning.~~

Baby Shower Invitation Idea
Here is a fun baby shower invitation idea to help cr
occasion.

Baby Shower Invitation
A great baby shower invitation for the internet age.

Baby Shower Invite
Since the baby shower invite is the grand introduct
with it.

Do those three articles on baby shower invitations really have useful, unique content without the fluff? If I was critiquing this site, this would be the kind of thing I would look out for in the sitemap, as clues of content problems.

What about these two pages found on the same site:

~~Many companies now offer beautiful satin baby shower invitations.~~

Baby Shower Invitations For Twins
Double the blessing and a baby shower invitations for twins should convey the excitement.

Twin Baby Shower Invitation
A twin baby shower invitation has the added feat of acknowledging more than one gender.

The reason webmasters do this is not for the benefit of the visitor. It's for the benefit of the search engine. They hope that each page will rank well for its variation of the phrase, and therefore bring a lot more traffic to the site than just one article optimized for one of the phrases.

So are they right, is this a good money-making strategy?

Well, it was once, but it's not today, although there seem to be a lot of webmasters who still live in the past for some reason. I'm not sure why because they're on a hiding-to-nothing the second they start writing content like this. Seriously, this type of keyword focused content will get your site into trouble with Google, so check through your sitemap to identify possible problems. You can combine similar articles into one piece, but make sure you cut out the fluff and make these articles the best that they can be.

- Titles & headlines

  The <title> tag is an important part of a webpage. It tells the visitor what the page is about (the title is often used in Google as the anchor text to the page). The headline on the page is also important for similar reasons. Google has traditionally used keywords in the title and headlines to help rank a page. And in case you're wondering, yes, webmasters have abused these areas – a lot!

Let's look now at the white-hat approach to titles and headlines.

1. You should write your titles for HUMANS, not for search engines.

2. You should write your headlines for HUMANS, not for search engines (are you seeing a pattern here?).

3. Your **headline** should be unique to the page it's on (not duplicated on other pages).

4. Your **title** should be unique to the page it's on (not duplicated on other pages).

In the past, one of the best ways to rank a page for a particular phrase was to use the exact phrase for the title and the opening headline. Of course, the same phrase would be sprinkled down the page as well, but the title and headline were the strong ranking factors. Today, this won't work (at least for the long-term), so don't use a single keyword phrase as either the title or the headline, or both. Titles and headlines should be crafted to draw the reader in. They can include topic-related phrases, but don't stuff, and above all else, **write them for humans**.

While we are on the topic of page titles, make sure that no two pages on your site share the same title. This also goes for Meta descriptions if you use them, and that includes a "template" description that just substitutes a word or phrase each time it's used (as is typical on doorway pages)..

- Written for the search engine or the visitor?

We've touched on this several times already, but it is so important that I am including it as a separate bullet point. Was the content written for human viewers or for the search engines? If the latter or you are just not sure, then that piece of content needs some work.

- Hidden text on the page?

One way that webmasters have tried to fool the search engines is with hidden text that contains keyword phrases. Hidden text can be achieved a few different ways, though the simplest is to use white text on a white background.

Fortunately, checking for hidden text is easy. Start by opening the webpage in a browser and then click on it somewhere. Now press CTRL+A (command + A on a Mac computer) to select everything on the page. All the page contents should now highlight (select), including any hidden text. Check to make sure that all text on the page is visible. Any hidden text that you find needs removing immediately.

- Visible blocks of text that are only there for the search engines.

An example of this is when a web page lists "incoming search terms", like this one:

Incoming search terms:

- food presentation ideas
- food presentation
- fruit decoration images
- funny food presentation
- fruit art with kids
- fruits foods pictures
- garnishing with vegetables
- picture of joke flower
- food wallpaper
- funny food garnish

What is the point of that list?
Does it in any way help the visitor?

Lists like this serve one purpose only, and that is to add keywords to the page to try to make it rank better in Google. Therefore, according to Google, it is spam.

Incoming search term lists are not the only type of block you'll find on web pages. On travel sites, I've frequently seen long lists of towns or cities. They are often not hyperlinked to relevant sections of the site, which suggests they only serve to add keywords to a page.

Any block of text on your page that is only there to increase keywords on that page, really does need removing ASAP.

- Over-optimization of the page as a whole.

Google has gone out of its way to stop webmasters over-optimizing their sites. This is because SEO is spoiling their otherwise great search results by showing pages that don't deserve to be at the top.

While a lot of over-optimization relates to the backlinks of a website (and we'll cover that later), it also applies to what is on the website itself.

Look at the pages on your site to see whether a single phrase is used more than you might expect, thus making it obvious the phrase(s) was an intended target. If you find any of these, also check to see whether:

- Links to that page are using that phrase as anchor text?

- Is that phrase also in key areas of your web page, like title, meta description, H1 header, opening paragraph, ALT tag, image title tags, bolded, italic etc.

As a General Rule, SEO Should Be "Invisible"

I don't mean that there is none, just that what is there should be discrete and not openly obvious or in-your-face.

There are WordPress plugins available, designed to help you check your on-page SEO. These are keyword driven checks and I think they are a bad idea. Content should NOT be keyword driven anymore, it should be visitor driven.

If you have been using an SEO plugin that checks for placement of keywords in an article, I'd recommend using it to de-optimize your articles (removing phrases from places they really don't need to be), and once you're done, delete the plugin.

- Is your content driven by keywords or by what the visitors want?

This is always a good check to make. Ask yourself whether the content you write on your site is driven by keyword research, or driven by what your visitors actually want to see.

I'm not saying you cannot use keywords in your content, of course you can. My point is this: instead of thinking you have to write an article about the phrase "tablet vs. laptop",

Keyword	Approximate CPC (Search) [?]
☐ tablet vs laptop ▾	€4.84

...just because it commands a high cost per click, consider writing an article on the "advantages and disadvantages of using a tablet instead of a laptop".

OK, it could be the same article right? However, thinking about your content in terms of the visitor, instead of your keyword research tool, should ensure your content has a fighting chance of pleasing Google. Of course, you could include the phrase "tablet vs. laptop" in your article if you wanted too, and as long as it made sense to do so and was not just squeezed into the content for the sake of it. I'm just suggesting a different approach to choosing the topics you write about, that's all. Many of us got into bad habits in the past – we had to - but the only way forward now is to replace old habits with new. Think what article the visitor wants to see first, then go and see which keywords and themed words are relevant to the article before you write it.

To quote the wise words of Dr. Wayne Dyer:

"Change the way you look at things, and the things you look at change."

- Does your content reflect search/visitor intent?

Does your web page offer a good match for the search terms that found it?

Here's an example to illustrate: Let's say you rank #1 in Google for the term "natural pain killers", but your web page only mentions one "natural" remedy in passing while discussing an array of more conventional, pharmaceutical pain killers. Is the visitor going to be happy with your page? I doubt it. For starters, they wanted pain killers plural, and secondly they wanted natural pain killers, yet your page is mostly about pharmaceutical pain killers, with just a quick mention on one natural alternative.

As we've seen, Google have ways of measuring how happy visitors are with your pages like bounce rate, time on site, social signals, visitor interaction and so on.

Therefore, it's important you don't try to rank for phrases that are a poor match for your content.

- Does your page provide something not already in the top 10?

Does your content provide something that is not already available in the top 10 of Google? If not, think about why it should replace one of those pages in the top 10 slots? What type of things can you add to your webpage to make it stand out from the rest? What can you include that the other top 10 pages don't offer?

Consider things like:

- Personal stories.
- Your own opinions.
- Your own unique thoughts, ideas etc.
- Images or photographs that work with the topic of the page.
- Visitor interaction – maybe a poll asking for visitors own opinions. A poll coupled with an active comments section creates a great resource, especially if the topic of your page was a little controversial.

Content Quality Checklist

Look at every page on your website. Use the following checklist to determine the quality of your content. Apply anything to your page that is missing.

- If the page is essentially an article, could it appear in a quality magazine?
- Is this the type of content that people would want to bookmark?
- Are people likely to share this content with their own friends and followers?
- Check a sentence or two in Google to see if your content is published (illegally or otherwise) on other websites. If it is, you need to implement Google authorship immediately and hope that they give you authorship of your own content. Also, contact any webmaster who is illegally displaying your content and ask them to remove it (see the article I linked to in this section of the book on copyright infringement).
- Is it a product review? If yes, is it unbiased? Does it tell of the good, the bad and the neutral? Does your review add information that gives opinions and views which are not found on the manufacturer's website, or any other website for that matter?
- If you use affiliate links, do your visitors know they are affiliate links? They

should do.

- Read each piece of content and look for keyword stuffing. Does it read naturally for a human, or was it written for a search engine? If any word or phrase appears more often than might be expected in a naturally written piece of content, then re-write it.
- How much "fluff" is in your article? Try to make sure your content does not contain fluff or watered-down filler text. Get rid of any sentences that are only there to increase word count. If you have to remove a lot of fluff, perhaps the article could benefit from a total re-write.
- Do any two (or more) articles overlap in terms of what they talk about? Do one or more other pages on your site repeat the same information? If yes, get rid of the duplication.
- Check your sitemap for possible problems. Are there any entries with similar filenames or titles that may indicate the articles cover the same/similar material? Are there any entries that suggest the content was written around keywords rather than around the interests of the visitor? If yes, get rid of (or re-write) all content that was not written specifically for visitors.
- Check all of your page titles and headlines to make sure you don't have the exact same title and headline on other pages. Headlines and titles should work together to entice the visitor. You should always write these for the visitor, and never for the search engines.
- Check Meta descriptions, if you use them. These should not be keyword stuffed. Once again, always write for the visitor, not the search engines, as a way to inform your visitors what the content is all about.
- Make sure you don't use the same Meta description (or "templated" description) on more than one page.
- Check each page for hidden text and remove any that you find.
- Are there any visible "blocks of text" on your pages that are only there for the search engines? If yes, get rid of them.
- SEO should be "invisible". Is it difficult to spot intentional SEO on your pages/site? It should be.
- Is your content driven by keywords or by what the visitor really wants to see? If the former, you need to clean up the content.
- Check to see what keywords visitors are finding your pages with. Does your page reflect the searchers intent for these keywords?
- Does your page provide something not found on any other website's web pages?

If you are interested in learning more about writing and developing quality content for your site, you can check out my book "Creating Fat Content", which is available on Amazon in Kindle and paperback format.

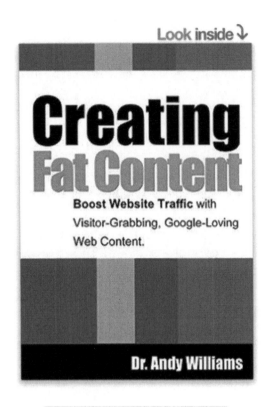

Look inside ↓

READ ON

Search Amazon for **BOOLTZMERM**

Creating Fat Content: Boost Web

by Dr. Andy Williams ▾ (Author)

★★★★★ ▾   16 customer reviews

▸ See all 2 formats and editions

Kindle $4.49	Paperback $9.99
Read with Our **Free App**	2 Used from $10.47
✓**Prime** Borrow for free ▾	4 New from $9.76

Back in 2007 I released a course called "Creating popular course ever. This book evolved from that reflect the huge changes made by Google in rec

Despite these changes, one thing has not chang best web pages to their users. But what constitut

▾ Read more

Length: 160 pages ▾

Checklist Point #10 – Inbound Link Profiles

Getting links pointing back to your website has always been one of the main jobs of any webmaster. Although Google doesn't like it, they did tolerate the behaviour, at least until they rolled out Penguin. Overnight, established websites dropped from the rankings. Pages that had been holding the top slot for years suddenly disappeared completely from Google's SERPs.

Google had done something that no-one believed they ever would. They started to enforce their guidelines relating to "link schemes".

Link schemes

Any links intended to manipulate PageRank or a site's ranking in Google search results may be considered part of a link scheme and a violation of Google's Webmaster Guidelines. This includes any behavior that manipulates links to your site or outgoing links from your site.

http://support.google.com/webmasters/bin/answer.py?hl=en&answer=66356

Any site that is seen to be participating in link schemes is in danger of a ranking loss. Even worse than that, any site that HAD participated in link schemes is also in danger. That means if you have a site that you are now running "by the book", but you had been involved in some dodgy link schemes in the past, your rankings could still be seriously affected if you never cleaned up those poor quality backlinks.

Google are constantly looking for unnatural link patterns. That is, links which have clearly been built by the webmaster, usually, though not always, on a large scale, and often of low quality.

To put it bluntly, **Google don't want you to build links to your own website**, at least not links whose sole purpose is to improve your rankings. As you look through your own backlink profile, it's important to be able to identify links that may be causing your site problems. If you do find any, deal with them accordingly. These include any links that Google would consider part of a "link scheme".

Before I go through the kinds of links that will hurt your site, let me be clear about one thing: If your site received a penalty because of its backlinks, cleaning up those backlinks WILL NOT return your site to the same "pre-penalty" rankings. The reason is that your pre-penalty rankings were achieved WITH the help of these spammy links because Google was still counting them back then. In other words, these spammy links were contributing to your success in the SERPs; the very reason why we used to build them. By removing them now means your pages won't have the same inbound links, and therefore won't rank as high. So, while cleaning up your links is vital to your long term success, don't expect that cleaning them up will put your old rankings back to where they were, because it won't. For that to happen, you'll need to build new, stronger, authority links to your site to replace the ones you've deleted/removed.

Ok, it's important to know first what constitutes a bad link. Before we look at that though, it's probably better that I tell you how to find the links that point to your site.

Finding Backlinks to Your Website

There are several tools you can use, some free, others paid. However, the one you should be using as part of your backlink search is Google Webmaster Tools, which is totally free.

Google Webmaster Tools

Google webmaster tools (https://www.google.com/webmasters/tools/home?hl=en)

If you don't have an account with Google Webmaster Tools, I recommend you create one right away. If Google wants to notify you of problems with your site (spiderability, spyware detected, links warnings, etc), they'll do it through Google Webmaster Tools (GWT).

GWT also shows you the links that Google know about.

Once logged in to GWT, go to the **Traffic** section in the sidebar, and then select **Links to your site**:

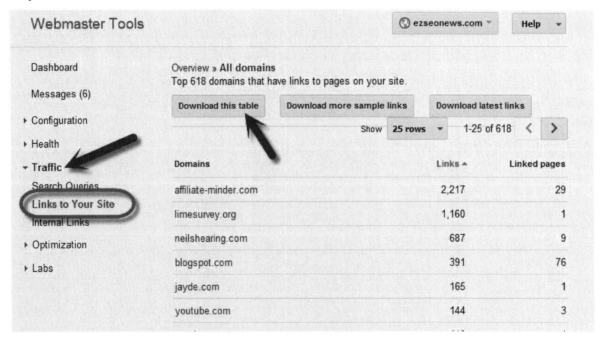

There is a link at the top of the table allowing you to download all of the links in that table. You'll get data on how many times a domain links to your site, and how many pages on your site it links to.

You can inspect the backlinks from any of these domains by clicking the hyperlink in the **Domains** column.

For example, in the list of domains pointing at my site, I didn't recognize a domain called **greenscapemedia.com.** I clicked the hyperlink to see what pages on my site it was linking to:

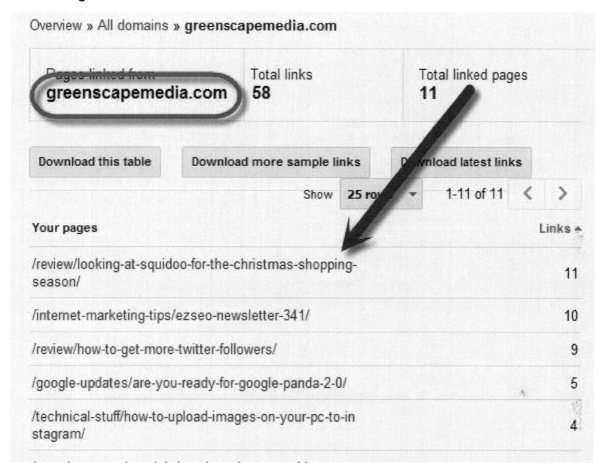

This screen tells me that greenscapemedia.com has a total of 58 links pointing to pages on my website.

The table lists my pages that the domain links to, and how many links point to each of these pages.

I can see that greenscapemedia.com links to 11 of my pages in total (the table tells me it's showing 1-11 of 11 pages).

From the links column on the right, I can see that this domain has 11 links pointing at the top URL, 10 pointing to the next, 9 to the next and so on.

I can view the URLs on greenscapemedia.com that link to any of my pages by clicking the URL hyperlink (arrow in the screenshot) for my page. If I check the links pointing to my "Squidoo for Christmas Shopping" post, I can see this:

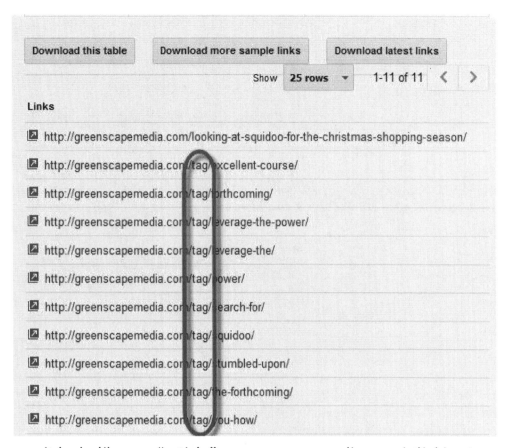

In this case, it looks like one "article" on greenscapemedia.com is linking to my page and the other 10 links are on tag pages. I'd guess that those tag pages are the various tags this webmaster used when tagging his main article. I can also see that this webmaster stole my article's title, and therefore probably part of my article too.

I can click these hyperlinks to open these pages in my web browser. This allows me to view the links to my site.

The URL at the top of this list is a basic spam page, and one that I would try to remove if my site had been penalized for dodgy backlinks.

I should now go back and check the 10 other pages on my site that greenscapemedia.com is linking to.

What I love about GWT is that you get to see the link data that Google has for your website. I'm sure they don't show you everything, but it really is a great start to see their backlink data. GWT is always my first stop to find any problematic backlinks.

SEO Spyglass

SEO Spyglass is a commercial tool, though there is a free version to get you started. The free version won't let you save your data and there may be other limitations, but it can find any links that don't get reported in GWT.

SEO Spyglass: http://www.link-assistant.com/seo-spyglass/

With SEO Spyglass you just type in the URL of your site and let the software do the rest. It goes off to numerous sources to find all the backlinks to your website.

SEO Spyglass gives you masses of information about the links to your site, things like:

- Which page it links to.
- The anchor text.
- Whether the link is dofollow or nofollow.
- IP address.
- Domain age.
- How many links per page.

And lots more besides.

SEO Spyglass really is a great tool for finding backlinks and specific link data for your site.

Ahrefs

This site is a popular one and for good reason. It does an excellent job of finding links to your website. The free version is very limited, so to get the best out of this tool you need a paid subscription.

Ahrefs: http://ahrefs.com/

Majestic SEO

Majestic SEO has a very useful free option. It also has more comprehensive paid plans for those who want additional features.

Majestic SEO: http://www.majesticseo.com/

To see what is included in the free version, visit this page:

http://blog.majesticseo.com/general/what-majesticseo-gives-you-for-free/

I recommend you sign up for a free account. Once you have done that, you can create a free report for your domain. This involves uploading a text file to your server (this proves the domain is yours). Once confirmed, Majestic SEO starts to analyse links to your domain. You'll then find the report in your reports screen. See the post above for a good introduction to using Majestic SEO. It includes an excellent video "webinar".

Ok, so you now know how to find the links. The next step in the process is to understand how to evaluate them.

Link Schemes

A Quote from Earlier:

> "Any links intended to manipulate PageRank or a site's ranking in Google search results may be considered part of a link scheme and a violation of Google's Webmaster Guidelines."

Link schemes include "any links intended to manipulate a site's ranking in Google search results".

Below are the schemes that can get you into trouble. You should check your site to make sure you are not engaging in any of these activities:

- **Buying or selling links that pass PageRank:** If your site has bought links, or sells links, then Google will probably come after you. Please note that when I say "buy", I don't necessarily mean that money changes hands. You could pay for a backlink in any number of ways, e.g. goods, services, free products, etc. If a webmaster has taken any kind of "reward" to host your links, then they are considered part of a link scheme. This even includes links found in product reviews, where you have given the webmaster a free copy of your product in exchange for the review and backlink.
- **Partner pages:** These were all the rage 10 years ago. You put up a partner page on your site and linked back to other websites in return for a link. These were commonly known as resource pages. Get rid of any links on a resource/partner page that are reciprocated, that is, those sites which link back to yours.
- **Linking to undesirable neighbourhoods:** If you link to any other site on the web, you are responsible for that link. Google sees links as votes for another website. So if you link to spammy websites, or even websites unrelated to your content, then be warned. You could easily get penalized for it.

One of the places where webmasters unknowingly link to these bad neighbourhoods is in the comments section of their website. When people leave comments, they often include their URL, which could end up as an active link in the comments section of your webpage. Even if the link looks good now, there is nothing to stop the author of that comment redirecting it later on. They might redirect it to a porn site, or another undesirable website that you would not want to be associated with. Because of this, I recommend you make comment links nofollow. At least this way you are telling Google that you don't necessarily endorse that link.

- **Automated backlinks:** Backlinks built in an automated fashion, using software and/or spun content, will cause you a lot of problems. Not only are the backlinks generated by these tools of low quality, they are also fairly easy for search engines to identify. If you have backlinks built in this way, try your best to remove them, and sooner rather than later.
- **Links in articles that you publish on other websites:** Be careful here. If the anchor text is clearly trying to manipulate the rank of your web page, Google will sport it. Google cites "large-scale article marketing or guest posting campaigns **with keyword-rich anchor text links**" as a problem, but then you should already know that by now, that's if you've read the preceding chapters.

Here is an example that Google uses within their guidelines:

> Links that are inserted into articles with little coherence, for example:
> *most people sleep at night. you can buy <u>cheap blankets</u> at shops. a blanket keeps you warm at night. you can also buy a wholesale heater. It produces more warmth and you can just turn it off in summer when you are going on <u>france vacation</u>.*

See how the anchor texts within the body of this piece are specific keyword phrases? These are clearly attempts to manipulate rankings, and Google will catch anyone who tries it.

If you write articles for other websites, say in the form of guest blogs, I recommend you use a resource box at the end of the article for pointing a link back to your homepage. Make sure you use either the site name, or site URL as the anchor text. If you want to include a link within the body of the article, then I advise you to use either the URL of the page you are linking to, or its title/headline as the anchor text. This approach is far more natural than keyword-focused anchor text.

- **Low quality links in general:** Google specifically mentions low-quality directory and bookmark sites.

I know there are a lot of tempting back-linking gigs on places like fivver.com, but don't use them. Once you have been submitted to hundreds of low quality directories or bookmark services, you won't be able to get those links taken down if you need to, meaning the damage is permanent.

Other types of low quality links include any type of "profile link" that is clearly only being used for the backlink.

Forum signature links that use a keyword phrase are also bad for your rankings. If you are a member of a forum and you want to include a link to your site in your forum signature, then use your site name or URL as the anchor text. Using a specific keyword phrase is clearly an attempt at trying to get your page to rank better for that phrase. Google's web crawling bot can easily detect this old hat approach to link building.

- **Theme & widget backlinks:** In recent years, another link-building "loophole" was to create a template, or maybe a WordPress widget/plugin, that would be given away for free, but there was a slight catch. Anyone using the theme or plugin would have a link inserted into their homepage (usually in the footer), back to the author's website. It was a simple reciprocal arrangement. You got something for free and all you were required to do was accept a little link that pointed back to the developer's own website. Google clamped down on this during 2012, and penalized a lot of websites.

- **Site-wide links:** We looked at this earlier in the book. Any links that appear on all the pages of your site are site-wide links. An example would be a blogroll, on a WordPress site. Blogrolls typically list links to "favourite blogs" in the sidebar. However, people buying site-wide links on other sites in the past have abused them greatly. Google hit back hard on this arrangement and penalised anyone who took part, especially on a large scale.

I know we all have navigation on our sites. We also place some items on every page of the site. However, pay particular attention to any site-wide links that use a keyword phrase as the anchor text. These are the ones which are more likely to get you into trouble. You know the type, links that read like "<u>make money online</u>" or "<u>buy cheap contact lenses</u>", typically found in the footers of all pages on your site. All site-wide links with keyword rich anchor text need looking at carefully and changing/removing wherever necessary.

As you can see, link building has just become a lot more difficult. If you listen to Google, they'll just tell you to write great content and the links will come naturally. Unfortunately, the people at Google seem far removed from the reality of the situation. Getting others to link to your content, no matter how great it might be, is not as simple as Google suggest. This is because webmasters are not so generous about linking out to other websites. We therefore do need to find ways to get backlinks that at least appear to be more natural. My companion book "SEO 2013 & Beyond" has ideas for these (see appendix at the back for details of my other books).

In terms of critiquing/cleaning up your backlink profile, your job is to try and identify your links and then clean up ALL the poor quality ones that point to your site. The next job is to then build new, better quality links to replace the ones you've removed.

Make a List of All Bad Links to Your Site

The first step to cleaning the links you have identified as "bad" is to contact each webmaster in turn, asking them to remove the offending link(s). Successful or not (and in most cases it won't be), document every attempt you make. When you have the data to show you have tried to clean up your backlinks, you can then approach Google using their Disavow tool:
https://www.google.com/webmasters/tools/disavow-links-main?pli=1

The disavow tool tells Google that you want these links ignored AND that you have tried to clean them up. There are no guarantees with the disavow tool, but it is well worth a go when you consider your final option, which is to move the site to a brand new domain and begin the back-linking process from scratch.

There is a good article here that describes one person's positive results using the disavow tool: http://www.seomoz.org/ugc/googles-disavow-tool-works-penalty-removal

Other Specific Things to Look Out for in Your Backlink Profile

1. **Diverse IPs:** Is there a good spread of IP addresses for the pages that link to

your website? A lot of links from the same or very similar IP addresses may indicate a blog network, or links from self-owned domains.

2. **Lots of links from the same domain:** These could indicate site-wide links that may need removing. If the site is an authority and you get traffic from that site, then you might want to leave those links intact. If they are site-wide, and on low quality domains, then get them removed.

3. **Too many keyword phrase anchor texts:** Google Penguin is looking at the anchor text of inbound links. If you have a lot of links with the exact same anchor text, then that is unnatural, and Google knows it. If it is the name of your site, then that's okay. If it is commercial keyword phrases that you want your site to rank for, then that's not okay. In 2012, anchor text links became a lot less important. My advice is to water these down significantly and aim for links designed to increase your authority, i.e., using your domain name, brand name or domain URL as the anchor text.

4. **Too many backlinks on low quality directories:** We mentioned this earlier so you know what to do here.

5. **Backlinks from spun content:** This is a huge problem if you have ever used automated backlink software to create backlinks using spun content. Spun content is one of the deadly sins of SEO. Google have been, and will continue to be, on the warpath for this. They are getting better and better at detecting it too. If you find backlinks in spun content, do your best to get them taken down. Sometimes this type of backlink is easy to spot by looking at the titles of the pages containing the backlinks. Here is an example of backlinks I found in GWT for one site that clearly used spun content for its backlinks:

Links

🔳 http://goarticles.com/article/Is-Serrapeptase-The-solution-to-Dupuytren-s-Disease/

🔳 http://goarticles.com/article/Serrapeptase-A-Feasible-Therapy-For-Numerous-Sclerosis/

🔳 http://goarticles.com/article/Serrapeptase-A-potential-Strategy-to-Multiple-Sclerosis/

🔳 http://goarticles.com/article/Utilizing-Serrapeptase-to-alleviate-Bodily-Discomfort/

This type of backlink is VERY bad for your site. Fortunately, these links were on the GoArticles website. I contacted them about the spammy nature of these articles and they promptly took them down.

Inbound Link Profile Checklist

Check the links pointing to your site using the tools mentioned in this book. If you only use one, then I'd recommend GWT.

Have you knowingly participated in link schemes? This includes:

- Buying or selling links to pass PageRank? (Get rid of paid links).
- Do you have a partner/resources page on your site containing reciprocal links? If yes, remove all reciprocated links.
- Are you linking (knowingly or unknowingly, perhaps via the comments system) to bad neighbourhoods? If yes, get all bad links removed from the comments.
- Do you have backlinks created by automated tools? If yes, try to get these taken down ASAP.
- Are backlinks pointing at your site from content that was spun? If yes, try to get the spun content taken down ASAP.
- Are there backlinks located in the body of articles which link to your site using keyword rich anchor text? If yes, I recommend you change these keyword links and use your domain name, brand name, domain URL or title/headline of the article, as the link text.
- Is there any low quality directory or bookmarking links pointing at your site? These will cause trouble if you cannot remove them. Add them to your list of links to disavow, if you eventually have to go down that path.
- Are there any backlinks to your site from themes or widgets that you have created? If yes, you need to deactivate those links.
- Are there any links on your website that link out to other websites from themes or widgets you may be using? If yes, remove them.
- Are there site-wide links pointing to your site from low quality websites? If yes, they need removing. Site-wide links from high quality websites are probably OK, and I wouldn't remove those except as a last resort.
- Are your links from a diverse range of IP addresses? If not, get more links from different IP addresses.
- Do you have links coming in from other websites that you own? If yes, are those links purely to help your pages rank better or is there a good reason to cross-link. If there is no good reason to cross-link the sites, remove those links.
- Are there lots of links from the same domain? If the domain is low quality, get them removed.
- Is there a high percentage of inbound links using keywords phrases you are/were targeting as anchor text? If yes, I'd advise you to water these down. Include more links that use the domain/brand name, URL or title/headline of the content you are linking to.

Real-World Examples of Bad SEO

Modern SEO is not just about keeping the search engines happy, it's primarily role is to keep your visitors happy. Their time on the site, including bounce rate and social interaction with your pages, are increasingly important signals that the search engines use to help decide how good your content actually is.

In this section, I want to highlight some examples of bad SEO that I found while critiquing a number of websites.

An Example of Bad Navigation

This was the sidebar on one website.

There are four sections to the navigation bar of this WordPress site.

The first section is the search box, which is a good thing. However, this is the default WordPress search box, which isn't such a good thing because it's pretty ineffective.

Under the search box is a section labelled "**Pages**". Pages in WordPress are one of two forms of content, the other being "Posts". This site seems to be mixing pages and posts in a way that makes me think the webmaster had no clear plan for the structure of the site. Either that or the project was built initially with pages, and then the webmaster later wanted to add more content and so decided upon posts.

My own advice is to restrict the use of Pages in WordPress to the "legal pages", and use posts for all content written for the visitor. There are of course some exceptions, but this is a good general rule, and one that allows you to make use of the excellent structural organization built into WordPress.

The next area of the navigation bar is an "Archives" section. What is the purpose of this? Does it help the visitor in any way?

If this site was news-based, where someone might like to check a news story from last week/month/year, then an archives section would be worth considering. However, this site isn't news-based. In fact it's a fairly static site with little or no new content being added. Therefore, the archives section just clutters and distracts an already cluttered and distracted navigation system.

The final area of the navigation menu is the "**Categories**" section. This is actually a useful section for visitors because they'll be able to find relevant POSTS. Note I put "posts" in capital letters. This is because PAGES won't be included in the category system (which only shows posts).

Search

Pages

- Depression Treatment Centers
- How to Deal With Depression
- Help for Depression
- How to Treat Depression
- Treatments for Depression
- Privacy Policy
- Contact
- Medical Disclaimer

Archives

- September 2011
- August 2011
- July 2011
- June 2011
- May 2011
- April 2011
- March 2011
- February 2011
- January 2011
- December 2010
- April 2010

Categories

- Help for Depression Tips and Strategies (12)
- Steps for How to Deal With Depression (8)
- Strategies for How To Treat Depression (1)
- Suffering From Depression Info (8)
- Treatments for Depression Discussion (9)
- Uncategorized (2)

Likewise, the PAGES listed in the top section of the navigation menu won't be found using the category menu at the bottom.

You can see how the navigation system on this site is not very well organized and only serves to confuse visitors.

Things actually get worse. This website has a sitemap, which you can see here:

URL		Priority	Change Frequency	LastChange (GMT)
http://	/	100%	Daily	2011-11-18 23:36
http://	/medical-disclaimer/	30%	Weekly	2011-11-18 23:36
http://	/contact/	30%	Weekly	2011-11-18 23:36
http://	/how-to-treat-depression/	30%	Weekly	2011-11-10 23:57
http://	/help-for-depression/	30%	Weekly	2011-07-01 23:44
http://	/how-to-deal-with-depression/	30%	Weekly	2010-12-18 17:49
http://	/depression-treatment-centers/	30%	Weekly	2010-12-18 17:45
http://	/treatments-for-depression/	30%	Weekly	2010-12-18 17:32
http://	/privacy-policy/	30%	Weekly	2010-12-15 20:50

Generated with Google Sitemap Generator Plugin for WordPress by Arne Brachhold. This XSLT template is released under GPL.

The sitemap only has nine entries, and that includes the homepage and three "legal pages". Only five content pages are included here, yet we can see from the sidebar navigation that this site has 40+ posts and a few content pages.

A sitemap should list ALL important URLs on the site, most notably the posts. Disclaimers and other "legal" pages can be left off the sitemap. The main role of the sitemap is to make sure the search engines can find the most important pages on your site. This one clearly misses the point.

Overall, the navigation system on this site (which I believe has now been taken down since I originally critiqued it for the owner), is a good example of what NOT to do.

If you would like to test out your SEO sleuthing skills, have a look at the pages in the sidebar menu (Pages section) and see another major mistake that this site made. Hint: Look at the page titles.

An Example of Over-optimization

Have a look at this web page:

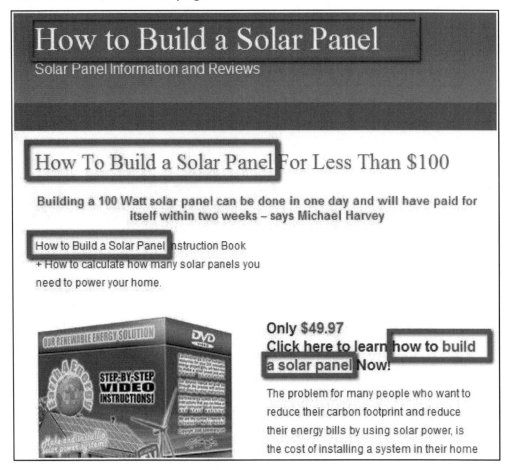

The webmaster was clearly trying to rank this page for "How to build a solar panel".

The top section of this page used the text "How to build a solar panel" in an H1 header. Then there is an opening H1 header which has the same phrase. That's two H1 headers on the same page, which is never a good thing. The exact same phrase then appears twice more, and this is all ABOVE THE FOLD. This phrase is also in the title tag of the page, and in the Meta description. It is also in the ALT text of an image on the page.

This is an extreme example of over-optimization.

Example of Fake Comments

Here are the comments on a website that I was critiquing:

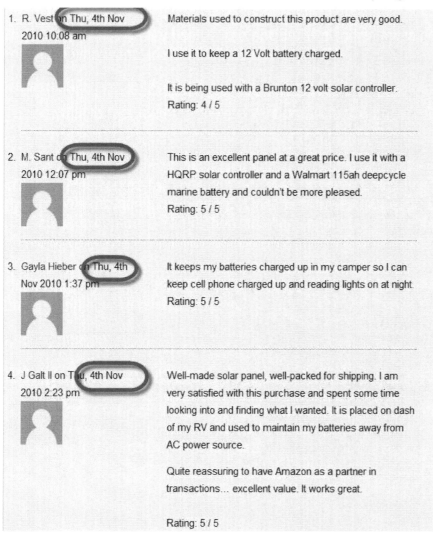

Notice that all of the comments were on the same day within just four hours of each other? That in itself is not unheard of, but the comments made me suspicious because they each included a high rating out of five (and none of them had Gravatar images).

To check the comments further, I took a sentence from one of them and searched Google for that sentence ("in quotes"):

"It keeps my batteries charged up in my camper so I can keep cell phone cl

Web   Images   Maps   Shopping   More ▾   Search tools

15 results (0.36 seconds)

Ad related to "It keeps my batteries charged up in my camper so I ... ⓘ
Ask an RV Tech Online - Technicians Will Answer in Minutes
rv.justanswer.com/Camper-RV
Questions Answered Every 9 Seconds.
Lawyer - Doctor - Nurse - Veterinarian

Amazon.com: Customer Reviews: HQRP 20W Mono-crystalline ...
www.amazon.com/HQRP-Mono-crystalline.../B002HT09TO
It keeps my batteries charged up in my camper so I can keep cell phone
charged up and reading lights on at night. Help other customers find the most
helpful ...

Amazon.com: HQRP 20W Mono-crystalline Solar Panel 20 Watt 12 ...
www.amazon.com › ... › Solar & Wind Power › Solar Panels
It keeps my batteries charged up in my camper so I can keep cell phone
charged up and reading lights on at night. Published on March 19, 2010 by Gayla ...

Amazon.com: Gayla Hieber's review of HQRP 20W Mono-crystalline ...
www.amazon.com/review/RW67BDW88G8WU
It keeps my batteries charged up in my camper so I can keep cell phone
charged up and reading lights on at night. Gayla Hieber March 19, 2010. Overall:
5.0 out ...

Looking for customer reviews for HQRP 20W Mono-crystalline Solar ...
askville.amazon.com › ... › Shopping › Lawn Garden
2 answers - 8 Jun 2011
It keeps my batteries charged up in my camper so I can keep cell phone
charged up and reading lights on at night. 4 of 4 found the following ...

Google found that exact same sentence/comment on 15 web pages, including Amazon.

Could the webmaster have found these comments on Amazon and added them to his website? Or maybe he paid someone else to add comments for him and they copied them from Amazon?

Whatever the answer is, this is bad.

I checked the other "fake" comments on the webpage and every one of them was on numerous other websites, including Amazon.

Example of Sneaky Affiliate Links

There is nothing wrong with having affiliate links on your website. However, visitors should know that they are affiliate links. Having "hidden" affiliate links that are designed to set a cookie is never a good idea.

One site I critiqued a while ago used the whole of the background of his site (all the space to the left and right of the main content) as one big affiliate link. Each time you clicked on the background you were directed, via an affiliate link, to the merchant site. This clearly is not a good idea. As I was critiquing the site, I cannot remember how many times I ended up on the merchant site. I can only guess at how annoyed visitors got with this. That was an extreme case.

Here is yet another case of hidden affiliate links:

Divine Baby Shower Cakes

The centerpiece of any party is a ... of whether to make o how much, can be difficult. Don't options available, you'll have a d

Beautiful Baby Shower Decor

Decorations are a vital part of an ... important because the set the tone for a party from the choosing a color set that works

Baby Shower Theme Ideas

It can be hard to decide on a the pamper the new mom with a trip diapers, onesies, and baby acce some of the ... below may ma

On this page, the webmaster had hyperlinked all of the images to Amazon with an affiliate link. The landing page was an Amazon search results page for the phrase **baby shower invitations**.

Why do this?
Does it in some way help the visitor?
Or is it an attempt to set a cookie on Amazon?

Of course, it could have been a genuine mistake, but this type of thing is not adding to the visitor experience one bit. Usually, when a visitor clicks on a thumbnail image they are expecting to see a larger image of that thumb, and certainly not whisked off to some other website.

An Example of How NOT to Create a Contact Us Page

On the contact page of one affiliate site I critiqued, I found this:

Contact Information

If you have any questions about satellite TV systems or service, please call DISH Network or DIRECTV's toll-free telephone number, or click on the link listed below.

DISH Network

For questions about DISH Network satellite tv systems or service, contact U.S. Dish:

By phone: 1-888-228-0942

Online: Click here for <u>U.S. Dish online support</u>

DIRECTV

For questions about DIRECTV satellite TV systems or service, contact U.S. Direct:

By phone: 1-866-529-6828

Online: Click here for <u>U.S. Direct online support</u>

Instead of contact details for the site, it provided contact details of two merchants instead. That meant visitors had no way to contact the actual webmaster of this website.

It also looks like this webmaster is pretending to be the merchant, or a website owned by the merchant.

Your contact page should give your visitors YOUR contact details so they can contact YOU. This not only builds trust, but is also a basic requirement of doing business online.

Incidentally, the same website also had a link in their menu labelled "Affiliate Information". This is typically something only found on a merchant site. On the Affiliate Information page, this website linked to the affiliate programs of the two merchants.

Example of a Bad Inbound Link Profile

Deciding what is a good or bad inbound link profile can prove challenging. What I mean by that is what does a natural profile look like anyway? Okay, how about this one?

Webpage PageRank	▾ %
PR: —	96.3% (1134)
PR: 1	1.6% (19)
PR: 0	0.8% (10)
PR: 3	0.8% (10)
PR: 2	0.3% (4)
PR: 4	0.0% (0)
PR: 5	0.0% (0)

These are links from PR1, PR2 and PR3 pages, which is good. However, these amount to just 2.7% of all inbound links. A whopping 96.3% of inbound links (that's 1,134 links) came from web pages where the Page Rank was N/A (the lowest possible rank, often found on very new pages, pages that have been penalised, or pages of very poor quality).

This profile indicates to me that the webmaster went for quantity, not quality, and from some very poor sources too. I'd expect to see this type of profile on a site that used automated back-linking software. This is exactly the kind of thing that Google Penguin will bite you for.

If this was my site, then I'd be looking at those 1,134 backlinks and deciding which ones to disavow. **I would not automatically disavow all of them**. Any links that appeared on poor quality, spammy web pages (or poor quality sites in general), would be added to my disavow list. However, remember that just because a page does not have demonstrable authority (in this case PageRank), does not necessarily mean it is a bad page. If the page your link is on looks good quality, and the site itself look quality, then leave those backlinks intact.

Example of Bad Internal Linking

The purpose of internally linking pages on a website is to help the visitor. When done correctly, it helps guide visitors to more information about certain topics.

On one website I critiqued, something strange was going on with the internal linking. Here are two examples of the type of internal linking I found:

ccount while others w only apply
res actual dollars for the **consumer**.

Finding the best credit card de for your spe
credit cards can often be a mplicated, confu
have little or **no experience** managing cards.

The anchor text in the first example was "consumer", and the anchor text in the second example was "no experience".

When you internally link pages on your site using contextual links, the anchor texts MUST relate to the pages they are linking to. The anchor text must also be fairly self-serving, not leaving anything to the imagination as to what the destination is about. I mean, what would a visitor think the destination URL is about if the link text is "consumer"? What about "no experience"?

The "consumer" link went to an article on "mileage credit cards".

The "no experience" link went to a page on "credit card debt relief".

Do these help the visitor? Nope! The only point I can think of is that the webmaster was trying to make sure their pages were crawled and indexed (and PageRank passed around), and so they added more links to them in this way.

Here is another one:

reveal a **secret weapon** that you can use aga
cuss this strategy, let us just look briefly at th
d companies to recruit you as their customer.

What has "secret weapon" got to do with any article on credit cards?

Do you see the problem with these?

One final example on this site is this internal link:

> ## 6. Borrow against your 401k
>
> When you **take a loan against your 401k** you are paying
> your goal is a one time payoff of credit card debt it can
> than to throw away 29% interest to a credit lending insti

The anchor text "take a loan against your 401k" linked to a page that did not include the word 401K!

The Complete Checklist

Checkpoint #1 - The Domain Name Checklist

- EMD? If yes, then be aware that this will work against you and you'll need to de-optimize the site for the phrase in the domain name.
- Is the EMD highly commercial in nature (not your brand)? If yes, then this might be a clear signal to Google that you are a spammer. The only option may be to move your site to a brand new domain.
- Is the domain name stuffed with keywords? If yes, there isn't much you can do with this other than to move the site to a better domain. Keyword stuffed domains look spammy and don't instil much confidence in visitors. Unless there is good reason to keep the domain, like it still makes good income or ranks well, then I'd seriously consider moving the site to a better, more brandable domain.

Has your domain ever ranked properly? If not, then check its history at the Way Back Machine. Consider submitting a reconsideration request to Google if the site looks like a poor quality, spammy project from the past.

Checkpoint #2 - Web Page Real Estate Checklist

- Resize your browser to 1024x768 and see what loads above the fold. Is the content useful? Are there too many adverts? If there are too many adverts, especially above the fold, consider removing (or moving) them.
- If you removed all of the adverts from the pages on your site, would those pages still offer the visitor what they are looking for? If not, then the content is not good enough.
- Does your site have sneaky links in the footer, especially keyword rich anchor text links, either to other pages on your own site or to external sites? If yes, then get rid of them.

Checkpoint #3 - Site Structure Checklist

- Is your navigation intuitive?
- Are all of the pages on your site just one or two clicks away from the homepage? They should be.
- Do you have site-wide links in the sidebar?
- Do you have site-wide links in the header?
- Do you have site-wide links in the footer?

NOTE: Site-wide links with keyword-rich anchor text are potentially the most damaging.

- If you have a large site, do you use dynamic menus, which change depending on the section of the site the visitor is viewing?
- Do you have a search box? If it is a WordPress default search box, I highly

recommend you switch to a more efficient script like Google's custom search.

- Do you internally link the pages of your website from within the body of your content, and not just via the navigation menus or a related posts menu?
- Is your content logically organized into "silos" where all related content is in the same category or folder? If necessary (e.g. on a large site), do you use sub-folders to help make the navigation even more intuitive?
- If you are using WordPress, do you have any tags that are only used once or twice? If so, remove them.
- If you are using WordPress, do you have any tags that are identical to some of your category names? If so, remove them. Never use a phrase for a tag if it is being used (or will be used) as a category.

Checkpoint #4 - Comments Checklist

- Does your website have a comments section where visitors can leave comments, thoughts and questions?
- Does your website have a Contact Us form?
- If you have comments enabled, are you manually approving all comments? You should be.
- Check through all of the comments on your site and remove any fake or spam comments. In fact, remove any comment where the sole purpose is to get a backlink to a website.
- Make comment links nofollow by default.
- Going forward, only approve legitimate comments where it is clear the visitor has read your content and added to the conversation with their insight.

Checkpoint #5 - Social Presence Checklist

- Does your website have a presence on Facebook?
- Does your website have a presence on Twitter?
- Does your website have a presence on Google plus?
- Does your website have social sharing buttons that allow your visitors to share your content with their own social media followers? Remember, you should include Twitter, Facebook and Google plus as a bare minimum.

Checkpoint #6 - The Trust Checklist

- Does the site have a photo of the webmaster/author of the content?
- Does your site have an About Us page?
- Are comments enabled?
- Does your site pretend to be a merchant?
- Is the author of your site a recognized authority in the niche/industry?
- Are you using a Gravatar set up on the email address that you use for your site?
- Does your site display your business address, preferably with a phone number?
- When was your site last updated?

- If appropriate, are there any testimonials and if yes, are they up to date?
- Does the copyright notice on your website display the correct year?
- Do you display any trust symbols (if appropriate)?
- Check all content for spellings and grammatical errors. Check your navigation systems for these errors as well.
- Are there any unanswered comments on your site?

Checkpoint #7 - Bounce Rate & Time on Site Checklist

Install Google Analytics and allow it to run for a few weeks so that you have sufficient data to work with. Once you're ready, check your bounce rate and time spent on site.

- Are your average bounce rates high?
- Are visitors spending a long or short time on your site?
- Look for specific pages where bounce rate is high AND time on site is low. Try to work out why these pages are suffering and fix them accordingly. Perhaps your page title does not accurately match the page content? This would mean that your listing in Google is misleading people to click through to your page, so when they do arrive there, they are disappointed and click the back button. Always consider tweaking page title and Meta description tags on any page with a high bounce rate, and then monitor the situation to see if your changes improve things.

Checkpoint #8 - Legal Pages Checklist

Not all of these pages are necessary for all types of website, so check which pages your site needs and add them if they are missing.

- Do you have a privacy page?
- Do you have a disclaimer page?
- Do you have a "terms of use" and conditions page (TOS)?
- Do you have a contact page?
- Do you have an about us page?
- Do you have a medical disclaimer page?
- Do you have an email policy page?
- Do you have an outbound link policy page?

Checkpoint #9 - Content Quality Checklist

Look at every page on your website. Use the following checklist to determine the quality of your content. Apply anything to your page that is missing.

- If the page is essentially an article, could it appear in a quality magazine?
- Is this the type of content that people would want to bookmark?
- Are people likely to share this content with their own friends and followers?
- Check a sentence or two in Google to see if your content is published (illegally or otherwise) on other websites. If it is, you need to implement Google

authorship immediately and hope that they give you authorship of your own content. Also, contact any webmaster who is illegally displaying your content and ask them to remove it (see the article I linked to in this section of the book on copyright infringement).

- Is it a product review? If yes, is it unbiased? Does it tell of the good, the bad and the neutral? Does your review add information that gives opinions and views which are not found on the manufacturer's website, or any other website for that matter?
- If you use affiliate links, do your visitors know they are affiliate links? They should do.
- Read each piece of content and look for keyword stuffing. Does it read naturally for a human, or was it written for a search engine? If any word or phrase appears more often than might be expected in a naturally written piece of content, then re-write it.
- How much "fluff" is in your article? Try to make sure your content does not contain fluff or watered-down filler text. Get rid of any sentences that are only there to increase word count. If you have to remove a lot of fluff, perhaps the article could benefit from a total re-write.
- Do any two (or more) articles overlap in terms of what they talk about? Do one or more other pages on your site repeat the same information? If yes, get rid of the duplication.
- Check your sitemap for possible problems. Are there any entries with similar filenames or titles that may indicate the articles cover the same/similar material? Are there any entries that suggest the content was written around keywords rather than around the interests of the visitor? If yes, get rid of (or re-write) all content that was not written specifically for visitors.
- Check all of your page titles and headlines to make sure you don't have the exact same title and headline on other pages. Headlines and titles should work together to entice the visitor. You should always write these for the visitor, and never for the search engines.
- Check Meta descriptions, if you use them. These should not be keyword stuffed. Once again, always write for the visitor, not the search engines, as a way to inform your visitors what the content is all about.
- Make sure you don't use the same Meta description (or "templated" description) on more than one page.
- Check each page for hidden text and remove any that you find.
- Are there any visible "blocks of text" on your pages that are only there for the search engines? If yes, get rid of them.
- SEO should be "invisible". Is it difficult to spot intentional SEO on your pages/site? It should be.
- Is your content driven by keywords or by what the visitor really wants to see? If the former, you need to clean up the content.
- Check to see what keywords visitors are finding your pages with. Does your page reflect the searchers intent for these keywords?

- Does your page provide something not found on any other website's web pages?

Checkpoint #10 - Inbound Link Profile Checklist

Check the links pointing to your site using the tools mentioned in this book. If you only use one, then I'd recommend GWT.

Have you knowingly participated in link schemes? This includes:

- Buying or selling links to pass PageRank? (Get rid of paid links).
- Do you have a partner/resources page on your site containing reciprocal links? If yes, remove all reciprocated links.
- Are you linking (knowingly or unknowingly, perhaps via the comments system) to bad neighbourhoods? If yes, get all bad links removed from the comments.
- Do you have backlinks created by automated tools? If yes, try to get these taken down ASAP.
- Are backlinks pointing at your site from content that was spun? If yes, try to get the spun content taken down ASAP.
- Are there backlinks located in the body of articles which link to your site using keyword rich anchor text? If yes, I recommend you change these keyword links and use your domain name, brand name, domain URL or title/headline of the article, as the link text.
- Is there any low quality directory or bookmarking links pointing at your site? These will cause trouble if you cannot remove them. Add them to your list of links to disavow, if you eventually have to go down that path.
- Are there any backlinks to your site from themes or widgets that you have created? If yes, you need to deactivate those links.
- Are there any links on your website that link out to other websites from themes or widgets you may be using? If yes, remove them.
- Are there site-wide links pointing to your site from low quality websites? If yes, they need removing. Site-wide links from high quality websites are probably OK, and I wouldn't remove those except as a last resort.
- Are your links from a diverse range of IP addresses? If not, get more links from different IP addresses.
- Do you have links coming in from other websites that you own? If yes, are those links purely to help your pages rank better or is there a good reason to cross-link. If there is no good reason to cross-link the sites, remove those links.
- Are there lots of links from the same domain? If the domain is low quality, get them removed.
- Is there a high percentage of inbound links using keywords phrases you are/were targeting as anchor text? If yes, I'd advise you to water these down. Include more links that use the domain/brand name, URL or title/headline of the content you are linking to.

Where to go from here

As you move forward in your SEO efforts, always:

Make sure that your site adds value. Provide unique and relevant content that gives users a reason to visit, bookmark and share your site.

In 2012, SEO changed forever. Google became far less tolerant of activities they see as rank manipulation. Google want to serve web pages that offer their visitors the best possible experience. That means your primary focus should be on your visitor, not Google, not a keyword research tool, and certainly not automated tools that claim to do your SEO for you.

As webmasters, we have been given a choice. Stick to Google's rules, or lose out on free traffic from the world's biggest search engine.

Sure, there will always be someone advertising the next greatest "loophole" to beat the system, and they'll even have examples to prove their loophole works. These examples may even go against everything that Google wants and break all the rules, which will make them tempting to some. However, these loopholes are short-lived. My advice to you is to ignore anyone that tries to sell you a loophole, a trick, or anything else that is "under Google's radar". If you want long-lasting results, stick to the rules - Google's rules.

The SEO in this book is the SEO I use on a daily basis. It's the SEO I teach my students, and it's the SEO that I know works. For those that embrace the recent changes, SEO has actually become easier as we no longer have to battle against other sites whose SEO was done 24/7 by an automated tool or army of cheap labor. Those sites have largely been removed, and that levels the playing field nicely.

Further Learning

If you like learning via video, I have a complete SEO course on Udemy. Normally that retails at $149, but for readers of my book, I have a special coupon code that gives you over 90% off. Here is the link:

http://ezseonews.com/SEOBOOK

I have a number of other courses on Udemy that you might be interested. You can find a list, plus coupon codes for all of them from my homepage: http://ezseonews.com/coupon-codes-for-all-of-my-udemy-courses/

NOTE: Use the first link above for a bigger discount.

For anyone interested in learning my own methods for building authority sites, backlinking and SEO in general, you can join my free internet marketing newsletter.

Finally I want to wish you good luck, and I hope that you enjoyed this book.

Please leave a review on Amazon

If you enjoyed this book, PLEASE leave a review on the Amazon website.

https://www.amazon.com/review/create-review?ie=UTF8&asin=B013F04FOI#

All the best

Andy Williams

My other Kindle books

All of my books are available as Kindle books and paperbacks. You can view them all here:

http://amazon.com/author/drandrewwilliams

Here are a few of my more popular books:

Creating Fat Content

Creating "Fat" Content that can rank and stick in Google

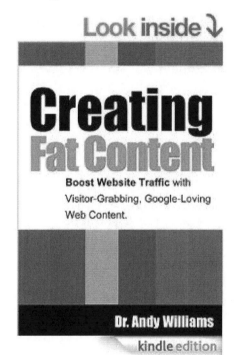

Google want to show the best web pages to their users, but what constitutes the "best"?

The answer is quite simple - the best content is the content that the visitors want to see.

Not very helpful? Then read this book. It's packed with advice on what Google actually want, and how you can deliver it with a simple mindset shift - by thinking in terms of "share-bait". That is, content that your visitors want to share with their friends, family and followers. Share-bait will put you on the right path to delivering content that keeps your visitors and search engines happy. It will give you an unfair advantage as your content has a better chance of not only ranking well, but sticking in the search engines.

Creating Web Content is a book packed with ideas, tips and strategies, for creating the most captivating, inspiring and fascinating content for your web site. By keeping your visitors happy, you won't have to worry about search engine algorithm changes, or Google slaps. The search engines will want to show your content to their users.

Search Amazon for **BOOLTZMERM**

Wordpress for Beginners

Do you want to build a website but scared it's too difficult?

Building a website was once the domain of computer geeks. Not anymore. WordPress makes it possible for anyone to create and run a professional looking website

While WordPress is an amazing tool, the truth is it does have a steep learning curve, even if you have built websites before using different tools. Therefore, the goal of this book is to take anyone, even a complete beginner, and get them building a professional looking website. I'll hold your hand, step-by-step, all the way.

As I was planning this book, I made one decision early on. I wanted to use screenshots of everything so that the reader wasn't left looking for something on their screen that I was describing in text. This book has plenty of screenshots. I haven't counted them all, but it must be close to 300. These images will help you find the things I am talking about. They'll help you check your settings and options against the screenshot of mine. You look, compare, and move on to the next section.

With so many screenshots, you may be concerned that the text might be a little on the skimpy side. No need to worry there. I have described every step of your journey in great detail. In all, this publication has over 35,000 words.

This book will surely cut your learning curve associated with WordPress.

Every chapter of the book ends with a "Tasks to Complete" section. By completing these tasks, you'll not only become proficient at using WordPress, but you'll become confident & enjoy using it too.

Search Amazon for **B009ZVO3H6**

Rapid Wordpress Websites

A visual step-by-step guide to building Wordpress websites fast!

Did you ever wish there was a tutorial that would show you just what you needed to know to create your first Wordpress website, without having to wade through stuff you'll never use?

Well this book is that tutorial. It teaches you on a strictly "need-to-know" basis, and will have you building your own website in hours. And I don't leave you stranded either. I created a companion website for readers of this book, with tutorials and help to take your Wordpress skills to the next level, when, and only when, YOU are ready.

What's in this book?

We start at the very beginning by getting good, reliable web hosting and choosing a domain name. I actually walk you through every step, so there will be no confusion.

Once you have your domain, we'll install Wordpress and have a look around the Wordpress Dashboard - think of this as your mission control.

After planning what we want to do, we'll actually build the companion site as we work through the book. We cover the essential settings in Wordpress that you need to know, how to use the editor, the difference between pages and post, categories and tags, etc.

We'll set up custom navigation so your visitors can find their way around your Wordpress site, and carefully use widgets to enhance the design and user experience.

Once the site is built, we'll play around with customizing the look and feel using themes, and I'll point you in the direction of some interesting plugins you might like to look at. These will be covered in more depth on the companion website.

The book will take you from nothing to a complete website in hours, and I'll point out a number of beginner mistakes and things to avoid.

Search Amazon for **B00JGWW86W**

Wordpress SEO

On-Page SEO for your Wordpress Site

Most websites (including blogs) share certain features that can be controlled and used to help (or hinder, especially with Google Panda & Penguin on the loose) with the on-site SEO. These features include things like the page title, headlines, body text, ALT tags and so on. In this respect, most sites can be treated in a similar manner when we consider on-site SEO.

However, different platforms have their own quirks, and WordPress is no exception. Out-of-the-box WordPress doesn't do itself any SEO favours, and can in fact cause you ranking problems, especially with the potentially huge amount of duplicate content it creates. Other problems include static, site-wide sidebars and footers, automatically generated meta tags, page load speeds, SEO issues with Wordpress themes, poorly constructed navigation, badly designed homepages, potential spam from visitors, etc. The list goes on.

This book shows you how to set up an SEO-friendly Wordpress website, highlighting the problems, and working through them with step-by-step instructions on how to fix them.

By the end of this book, your WordPress site should be well optimized, without being 'over-optimized' (which is itself a contributing factor in Google penalties).

Search Amazon for: **B00ECF70HU**

Kindle Publishing - Format, Publish & Promote your books on Kindle

Why Publish on Amazon Kindle?

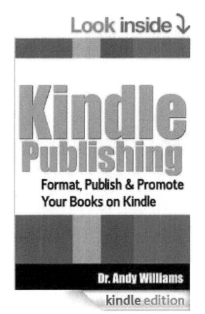

Kindle publishing has captured the imagination of aspiring writers. Now, more than at any other time in our history, an opportunity is knocking. Getting your books published no longer means sending out hundreds of letters to publishers and agents. It no longer means getting hundreds of rejection letters back. Today, you can write and publish your own books on Amazon Kindle without an agent or publisher.

My own success with Kindle Publishing

As I explain at the beginning of this book, I published my first Kindle book in August 2012, yet by December 2012, just 5 months later, I was making what many people consider being a full time income. As part of my own learning experience, I setup a Facebook page in July 2012 to share my Kindle publishing journey (there is a link to the Facebook page inside this book). On that Facebook page, I shared the details of what I did, and problems I needed to overcome. I also shared my growing income reports, and most of all, I offered help to those who asked for it. What I found was a huge and growing audience for this type of education, and ultimately, that's why I wrote this book.

What's in this Book?

This book covers what I have learned on my journey and what has worked for me. I have included sections to answer the questions I myself asked, as well as those questions people asked me. This book is a complete reference manual for successfully formatting, publishing & promoting your books on Amazon Kindle. There is even a section for non-US publishers because there is stuff there you specifically need to know. I see enormous potential in Kindle Publishing, and going forward, I intend to grow this side of my own business. Kindle publishing has been liberating for me and I am sure it will be for you too.

Search Amazon for **B00BEIX34C**

Self-Publishing on Createspace

Convert & Publish your books on Createspace

Self-publishing your own work is easier than at any time in our history. Amazon's Kindle platform and now Createspace allow us to self-publish our work, with zero costs up front.

Createspace is a fantastic opportunity for writers. You publish your book, and if someone buys it, Createspace print it and send it to the customer. All the author needs to do is wait to be paid. How's that for hands-free and risk-free publishing?

This book takes you step-by-step through my own process for publishing. Topics covered include:

- Basic Text Formatting

- Which Font?

- Links and formatting checks

- Page Numbering in Word

- Adding a new title to Createspace

- Price calculator and deciding on Trim size

- Image DPI requirements

- Paint Shop Pro conversion process

- Common formatting problems

- Book Cover Templates

- Creating the cover with Photoshop Elements

- Creating the cover in Paint Shop Pro

- Submitting the book & cover to Createspace

- Expanded Distribution?

The book also includes links to a number of video tutorials created by the author to help you understand the formatting and submission process.

Search Amazon for **B00HG0GE0C**

CSS for Beginners

Learn CSS with detailed instructions, step-by-step screenshots and video tutorials showing CSS in action on real sites

Most websites and blogs you visit use cascading style sheets (CSS) for everything from fonts selection & formatting, to layout & design. Whether you are building WordPress sites or traditional HTML websites, this book aims to take the complete beginner to a level where they are comfortable digging into the CSS code and making changes to their own site. This book will show you how to make formatting & layout changes to your own projects quickly and easily.

The book covers the following topics:

- Why CSS is important
- Classes, Pseudo Classes, Pseudo Elements & IDs
- The Float property
- Units of Length
- Using DIVs
- Tableless Layouts, including how to create 2-column and 3-column layouts
- The Box Model
- Creating Menus with CSS
- Images & background images

The hands on approach of this book will get YOU building your own Style Sheets from scratch. Also included in this book:

- Over 160 screenshots and 20,000 words detailing ever step you need to take.
- Full source code for all examples shown.
- Video Tutorials.

The video tutorials accompanying this book show you:

- How to investigate the HTML & CSS behind any website.
- How to experiment with your own design in real time, and only make the changes permanent on your site when you are ready.

A basic knowledge of HTML is recommended, although all source code from the book can be downloaded and used as you work through the book.

Search Amazon for **B00AFV44NS**

Migrating to Windows 8.1

For computer users without a touch screen, coming from XP, Vista or Windows 7

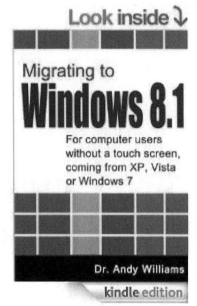

Review: "What Microsoft should buy and give away now to drive sales"

New PCs are coming pre-installed with Windows 8, Microsoft's new incarnation of the popular operating system. The problem is, the PCs it is installed on are not usually equipped with the piece of hardware that Windows 8 revolves around - a touch screen.

Windows 8 is probably the least user-friendly version of the operating system ever released. It's almost like two different operating systems merged together. From the lack of a start menu, to features that only really make sense on a tablet or phone, Windows 8 has a lot of veteran Windows users scratching their heads. If you are one of them, then this book is for you.

After a quick tour of the new user interface, the book digs deeper into the features of Windows 8, showing you what everything does, and more importantly, how to do the things you used to do on older versions of Windows. The comprehensive "How to" section answers a lot of the questions new users have, and there's also a complete keyboard shortcut list for reference.

If you are migrating to Windows 8 from XP, Vista or Windows 7, then this book may just let you keep your hair as you learn how to get the most out of your computer. Who knows, you may even get to like Windows 8.

Search Amazon for **B00CJ8AD9E**

You can find all of my books here:

http://www.amazon.com/Dr.-Andy-Williams/e/B00A0H8AY6/ref=dp_byline_cont_book_1